25

BICYCLE TOURS
in the Adirondacks

Distributed by
Lake Champlain Publishing Co.
Burlington, Vermont 05401
800-845-0028 • lakechamplainpub.com

Whiteface Mountain with Ausable River off NY 86. See Tour 7. (*Photo by Darren McGee, NY State Dept. of Economic Development*)

25

BICYCLE TOURS
in the Adirondacks

road adventures in the east's largest wilderness

Bill McKibben
Sue Halpern
Mitchell Hay
Barbara Lemmel

photographs by the authors

Backcountry Publications
Woodstock, Vermont

An invitation to the reader

Although it is unlikely that the roads you cycle on these tours will change much with time, some road signs, landmarks, and other items may. If you find that such changes have occurred on these routes, please let the authors and publisher know, so that corrections may be made in future editions. Other comments and suggestions are also welcome. Address all correspondence to:

Editor, 25 Bicycle Tours™ Series
Backcountry Publications
PO Box 748
Woodstock, Vermont 05091

Library of Congress Cataloging-in-Publication Data

25 bicycle tours in the Adirondacks : road adventures in the East's
   largest wilderness / Bill McKibben ... [et al.] ; photographs by the
   authors.

     p.   cm.
     ISBN 0-88150-318-5
     1. Bicycle touring—New York (State)—Adirondack Mountains—
Guidebooks. 2. Adirondack mountains (N.Y.)—Guidebooks.
   I. McKibben, Bill.
GV1045.5.N72A352   1995
796.6'4'097475—dc20   95-5912
                                                     CIP

10 9 8 7 6 5 4 3

Third Printing 1999

Printed in the United States of America

Cover and text design by Sally Sherman

Cover photo by Nancie Battaglia

Interior photographs by the authors

Maps by Dick Widhu, ©1995 The Countryman Press

Published by Backcountry Publications, a division of The Countryman Press, PO Box 748, Woodstock, Vermont 05091

Distributed by W. W. Norton & Company, Inc., 500 Fifth Avenue, New York City, New York 10110

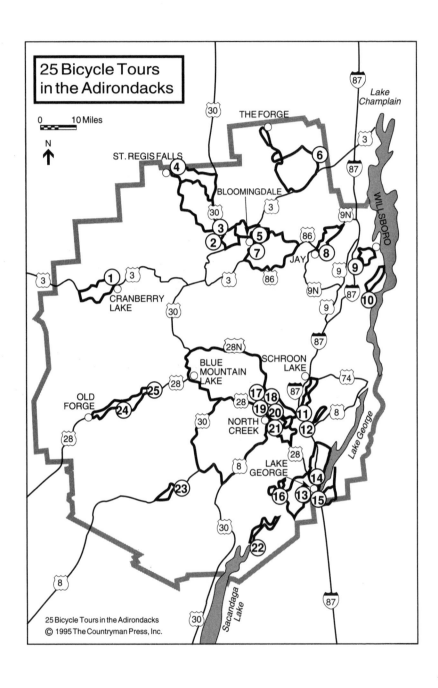

25 Bicycle Tours in the Adirondacks

© 1995 The Countryman Press, Inc.

Contents

Introduction

The Adirondack Park of upstate New York is the greatest wilderness east of the Mississippi. It covers 6 million acres—an area slightly larger than either Vermont or New Hampshire. Nearly half that land is "forever wild" under the state constitution—not a stick of timber can be cut. As a result, it is justly famous among backpackers, canoeists, cross-country skiers, hunters, anglers, and others who crave the wilderness.

It is less well known among bicyclists, and for some of the same reasons. Because of the great expanses of wilderness, there are very few roads in the core of the Adirondacks. Whereas neighboring Vermont, with its predominantly agricultural history, has a fine network of roads for hauling crops, the Adirondacks boomed in the days of heavy logging around the turn of the century. Most of the wood came out by river or railroad, so it is difficult, in the central mountains, to find short loops. And it is nearly impossible to find flat short loops—these are mountains, after all, and some of the most precipitous in the East.

You will notice, therefore, that many of the routes in this book are on the fringes of the mountains: in the gorgeous and rolling Champlain Valley, in the lake country north of the High Peaks, among the lakes and forests of the less-steep southern Adirondacks. Even so you will be in the wilderness most of the time, often riding roads lined with trees. The serendipity of Adirondack cycling has much to do with this wilderness—with the chance of seeing deer or moose, owl or hawk, coyote or fox on the edge of the vast tracts of forest preserve. And in many cases we have recommended hikes that can be combined with these rides to afford a vista of the area you have been riding in. (A key resource for really exploring the mountains is the exhaustive *Discover the Adirondacks* series of trail guides prepared by Barbara McMartin.) If you are susceptible to the charms of wilderness—if you want to ride for miles past places with no houses or signs, just rivers and forest—then, like us, you will find the Adirondacks to be paradise.

The wild character of this place influences bike touring in other ways as well. Though the Adirondacks are as large as Vermont, the park's population is barely one-sixth the size: Instead of small towns every half hour or 45 minutes, there are often long pushes between civilization—and civilization, when you finally get there, may be one small diner or a seasonal grocery store. Bike repair shops are about as common as palm trees in these latitudes. You will notice that we have tried hard to group rides around various nodes: Saranac Lake, North Creek, Lake George, and so forth. These places are large enough to have motels and campgrounds, and so serve as fine hubs for several days of bike riding. We have also tried to warn you at the beginning of each description if there are few or no stores along the way. It is best to carry with you everything you need for regular repairs, as well as plenty of food. It is possible, with careful planning, to do inn-to-inn treks in a few parts of the Adirondacks, but do not take for granted that you will find a place to stay in the next town on the map.

Because there are so few roads, those that do exist are sometimes heavily traveled. Please be very careful, especially where shoulders are narrow. Pavement is often frost-heaved and bumpy, and downhills can be treacherous. Some of these trips, because of the lack of roads, travel some distance on dirt. We have flagged these routes in the opening descriptions, and if you are on a skinny-tired and finicky racing bike you may want to skip them. Sturdier bikes are ideal for these mountains—two of us ride road bikes or a road tandem, and the other two are on mountain bikes or hybrids. Whatever you're riding, the more gears the better.

If you plan to combine your road-riding with some actual mountain-biking, the Adirondacks offers one of the largest single-track networks in the East. More than half the public land in the park is classified as "wild forest," and all the trails on it are open to bikes. Land designated "wilderness" by the state is closed to bikes, which is appropriate—this land is primarily for animals and plants, and if you want to experience it, go quietly, and on foot. These are among the oldest mountains on Earth, after all, and merit your respect. (The igneous and metamorphic bedrock underlying the Adirondacks is estimated to be a billion years old, though the rock faces we see are, geologically speaking, a mere ten thousand years old.)

The Adirondacks are rugged terrain in other ways as well. Winter comes very early—in the High Peaks, snowfall in late September is the norm, though the cycling season is extended much longer in the gentle farming country of the Champlain Valley. In the spring, there's often a lovely month of cycling beginning in mid-April (though watch carefully for the sand on the road left over from winter's plowing), and then 8 weeks or so of blackfly season. Blackflies do not make riding impossible; they do make slow riding uncomfortable. Think of them as personal trainers, pushing you to your peak performance.

Despite all the physical challenges, we think the Adirondacks is one of the great undiscovered biking areas of the East. If you want tough rides, you can find them (and outside the town of Lake Placid you're likely to be passed by Olympic athletes pedaling to keep in shape for cross-country skiing or speed-skating). If you love vistas, we've managed to find a few rides offering unparalleled views. And if solitude seems elusive at home, then the Adirondacks is the perfect destination: a charmed place, out of time, removed from the main current of human affairs, plugged in to the eternal current of the natural world.

A few general hints to make your bike-touring more comfortable and safe:

1. Wear a helmet. Wear a helmet. Wear a helmet. It might be possible to say this too often, but we don't think so: Wear a helmet.
2. Check your bike before beginning. Wheels secure? Brakes working?
3. Use a rearview mirror, either on your helmet or on your handlebars. Before you swerve, make sure you're not swerving in front of something—cars have gotten steadily quieter over the years and can sneak up on you.
4. Make sure you and your bike have reflective tape or patches, in case you slow down on the last 15-mile stretch and get caught out after dark. Bright-colored clothing is a good idea too. Also have a bike light.
5. Watch for the road surface. Newly laid pavement is a rare treat. More likely you'll find cracks, potholes, and patches—often patches on top of patches. Downhill is especially dangerous. Watch out for sand, left by spreaders in winter. In town, avoid storm sewers with grates running parallel to the road—they have been specially sized to nab bike tires. For the same reason, do not ride diagonally across railroad tracks. Walk your bike across, or make sure you approach at a right angle.

6. Dirt roads are for bikes with knobby tires. Smooth tires won't help you in sand. Wet leaves are slippery too—and there are more than a lot of leaves in the Adirondacks. Also be especially careful on steel-deck or wooden bridges, and any other funky surfaces.

7. Ride with traffic. And obey all the traffic signs. If cars are supposed to stop or yield, so are bikes. When you are turning, use hand signals. It's also a fine idea to ride with a bright orange bike flag so drivers will know where you are from a distance.

8. If you're resting or changing a tire, get all the way off the pavement.

9. Dogs are the only dangerous animals you're likely to encounter, and even they can usually be outrun—if you're spinning your pedals fast, they'll have a hard time chomping on your leg. There are commercial repellent sprays available, but a quick squirt from your water bottle usually works just as well.

10. Watch out for cars pulling in and out of stores and restaurants, and for car doors opening in villages. Riding with a radio or headphones is a big mistake—you need to be much more vigilant than you would be in a car. Remember: They haven't built a bike yet with an airbag.

11. Ride single file, not abreast. And stay a good distance apart as you ride, especially going downhill, so a spill doesn't turn into a multi-vehicle pileup.

12. John Freidin, the dean of Northeast bike-tourers, and author of *25 Bicycle Tours in Vermont,* urges that riders always dismount to make a left turn, and we consider it good advice as well.

13. Freidin adds this caution: "Always ride as if a lethal hazard lies just ahead, out of sight. Although the text mentions many potential dangers, it must not be relied upon as the final word, for road and traffic conditions constantly change. Use this book to find your way and increase your pleasure; rely only on yourself for your safety."

There are also some general tips that will make your cycling more pleasant. Some are obvious: If you haven't ridden for quite a while, start with the short and easy tours. Others are more technical, and open to some disputation, but we think you're better off with a firm seat, not one of the more tempting mushy models. Adjust your seat to the right height: When you are pedaling, the leg that is pushing down should be slightly bent at the bottom of its cycle.

When pedaling, don't try to push along in the highest gears: Lower gears are less tiring, and much easier on the knees. Eighty or even ninety revolutions a minute of the pedals is not excessive, and will leave you feeling fresher at tour's end than fewer revolutions on stiffer gears. Pedal with the balls of your feet, not your heels or your arches. Toe clips make it easier to get full power from your pedaling stroke, but make sure you can disengage your feet quickly if need be.

When you're going uphill, don't wait until you're struggling to shift gears—try to maintain the same rate of pedal revolutions, by shifting to a lower gear each time it starts to feel hard. If the hill is long and steep, drop down into your granny gear (the very lowest) and stay there, patiently plodding your way up the hill. Or get off and rest. There is no shame in dismounting; everyone does it.

It is as important to keep your body in good shape as your bicycle. Don't wear cotton—it will soak up sweat or rainfall and chill your body. Hypothermia is not unheard of in these mountains. Instead, wear one of the wicking synthetics. Padded bike shorts and tights are excellent, and many people find that padded biking gloves are useful. In windy or chilly weather, which is to say all but 4 or 5 days a year, windbreakers and waterproof clothing are essential as well.

Some things you will want to bring with you:

1. A helmet. Did we mention this before? We did. With good reason.
2. A handlebar bag, big enough to hold the rest of the items mentioned here. If you can find the kind with a transparent map pocket on top, so much the better—you may want to photocopy or clip out the maps in this book, or fold the book over. We'd also recommend carrying another map of whatever area you are in, in case you get lost or some of the roads we mention are closed.
3. A pump, a spare tube, and enough know-how to use them. We'd also include some basic tools: tire irons (or tire plastics, as they really should be called now), an adjustable crescent wrench, metric Allen wrenches, screwdrivers, and so on. With few exceptions, these rides are distant from bike shops. It makes excellent sense to know how to fix your own flats and do other minor repairs.
4. Food and water. Plenty of food and water. The store mentioned in the route may have gone out of business (a common Adirondack occurrence) or be closed for fishing. So bring fruit, bring sandwiches, bring

a candy bar to give you a last burst of energy, bring Powerbars. And bring water, water, water. Not one but two water bottles if you can manage it. (And remember not to drink straight from Adirondack streams or lakes. Giardia—the "beaver fever" bug—is widespread in the area and will cause you untold grief should you ingest contaminated water.) Remember not to wait until you are hungry to eat or thirsty to drink—keep your tank topped up at all times. And don't wait until you are falling over to rest. A series of short rests—5 or 10 minutes—will allow your body to recover but not give your muscles time to knot up.

5. A bike computer, which will tell you how far you're going (and how fast as well). These are cheap and simple, and having one will make using the directions in this book easier. Remember, however, that your readings are unlikely to be exactly like ours—the bike computer is not an infallible instrument. Use your judgment and your maps to supplement it, and when in doubt ask directions.

6. A bike lock. Bike theft is not common here, but you will have more peace of mind as you hike or eat your lunch if your bike is secured with a good lock such as a Kryptonite.

7. Safety equipment: Helmet. Rearview mirror. Bike lights and reflective patches or bands.

There are a few additional resources that will make your trip more enjoyable. Get a copy of the *New York State Atlas and Gazetteer* from DeLorme Publishing Co. in Freeport, Maine. It's available at most gas stations, and it divides the whole state into a series of topo maps that show most every detail. Keep it in your car, and outline the routes we suggest. Often you'll be able to see deletions and additions.

The Adirondack Book, by Elizabeth Folwell, is the best general guide to restaurants, motels, campgrounds, scenic attractions, antiques shops, crafts fairs, and the like. It too is widely available at gas stations and bookstores.

Discover the Adirondacks, volumes 1–11, a comprehensive masterpiece by Barbara McMartin, details nearly every possible hiking trail in the whole park. Find the one for the region to which you are heading; it will make your vacation infinitely richer.

Bike-touring pamphlets are available from the New York State Department of Environmental Conservation and the State Department of

Transportation, local tourism officials, and some bike shops; we have drawn on these resources, and on the knowledge of many park residents and friends, including Jim Gould, Jim Tucker, Brian Delaney, John Nemjo, Sam Allison, Chris Shaw, and Sue Kavanaugh.

Thanks, finally, to Ruth Sylvester and Carl Taylor at Countryman Press for guiding us along the high peaks of book publishing.

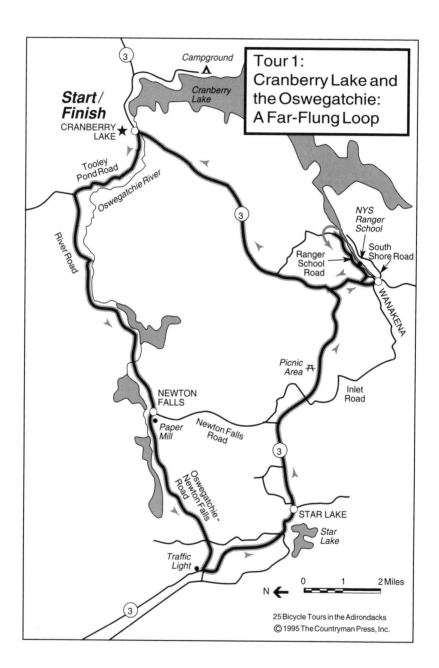

Tour 1:
Cranberry Lake and
the Oswegatchie:
A Far-Flung Loop

Campground

Cranberry
Lake

Start/
Finish
CRANBERRY
LAKE

Tooley
Pond Road

Oswegatchie River

River Road

NYS
Ranger
School

Ranger
School
Road

South
Shore Road

WANAKENA

Picnic
Area

Inlet
Road

NEWTON
FALLS

Paper
Mill

Newton Falls
Road

Oswegatchie-
Newton Falls
Road

STAR LAKE

Star
Lake

Traffic
Light

N ⟵

0   1   2 Miles

25 Bicycle Tours in the Adirondacks
© 1995 The Countryman Press, Inc.

16

1
Cranberry Lake and the Oswegatchie:
A Far-Flung Loop

Distance: 35.1 miles (This includes a 5-mile loop to the Ranger School at Oswegatchie, which can easily be eliminated.)
Terrain: Moderately hilly

No place in the Adirondacks is very near anything, something that is especially true of the Cranberry Lake region. North and west of the population centers of the park, it's one of those places where you can spin your radio dial and pick up almost nothing but static. (Not entirely true —the bottom of the FM dial is the province of North Country Public Radio, offering nice music and as reliable a weather forecast as you're going to get, from St. Lawrence University in Canton.)

Cranberry Lake is the third largest body of water in the Adirondacks. It's twice the size it used to be—the state legislature authorized a dam on the Oswegatchie in the 1860s that created a shoreline 160 miles long, with all the strange fingers and bays that mark a dammed lake. But if that makes this sound like a civilized place, it shouldn't.

The lake is bordered by the Cranberry Lake Wild Forest and the Five Ponds Wilderness—the latter includes the largest patch of old-growth forest in the eastern United States, with some massive virgin pine. These areas are not easy to get to—Barbara McMartin's *Discover the Northern Adirondacks* is an essential reference for anyone wanting to combine some hiking with their bike-touring. If you explore this backcountry, you are following in large footsteps—Bob Marshall, the founder of the Wilderness Society and the driving force behind the American wilderness movement, did some of his earliest bushwhacking in the area. Betsy Folwell, writing in *Adirondack Life,* described his hiking style thusly: "To flail around in the brush for hours and miles, maybe finding his destination, maybe not."

17

But you are booming along on nice pavement. There's plenty of scenery to see from the roads, and it's not hard to appreciate. Fredric Remington used to vacation in the region, and there's a definite Western, and Canadian, feel to the lonely landscape. Everything happens on a big scale—the great windfall of 1845, an inland hurricane, leveled a swath 100 miles long and 5 miles wide; a forest fire in 1908 cleared another huge area (much of which soon became state land).

There are a number of small towns and settlements along this route, so provisions should not be a problem. (Bike repairs are another story.) But you are on the very edge of the settled world as you pedal this tour. If wilderness attracts you, you will come back to the Oswegatchie region again and again.

0.0 *Beginning at the intersection of Tooley Pond Road and NY 3, just north of the Mobil station outside of Cranberry Lake, turn right onto Tooley Pond Road.*

0.3 *Water is visible on the left, the first of a number of openings to dammed-up and widened sections of the Oswegatchie River. Parts of the Oswegatchie, especially upstream of Inlet, are prime canoe water—this is flatter and more placid.*

0.8 *Cranberry Lake cemetery, a small and peaceful spot.*

1.2 *The road turns briefly to dirt, at least in 1994—but apparently it will be repaved in the future.*

1.75 *The road crosses a bridge over a tributary of the Oswegatchie.*

2.6 *The Windfall House Bar and Restaurant, a good family restaurant featuring a salad bar, commemorates in its name the 1845 windstorm that helped shape the forest ecology of the area.*

2.8 *Left on River Road, following signs to Newton Falls.*

The pavement is broken in places, but not hard to navigate, as you wind through a nice maple woods.

4.3 *Broad glimpses of water begin to appear, with lots of places to stop and picnic, fish, swim, and even launch boats.*

In many places you can see the stumps where the river drowned forests after it was dammed.

7.5   Small boat launch.

7.8   A steel-deck bridge takes you across the Oswegatchie, which is now on your right.

8.4   A parking turnout to the left and a sandy beachlike area on the right offer a prime lunching spot.

9.1   As you enter Newton Falls, turn right down the hill toward the paper mill, which produces a high grade of magazine paper. Continue along the road to the west. (This is NY 60, the Oswegatchie–Newton Falls Road, but it may not have a street sign.)

10.4 A long, gradual uphill begins.

The pavement on this road is good. While there is little shoulder, there aren't many cars.

11.7 The uphill ends, and a 2-mile descent begins.

13.7 At the blinking red light, turn left onto NY 3.

A 2-mile, fairly steady climb begins shortly after turning onto NY 3. You're halfway up it when you cross under a railroad bridge. This is a busier road but with a wide shoulder—in many places wide enough for two-abreast riding. If you need a soda, there's a Citgo station a few hundred yards to the right here.

15.7 The climb ends, conveniently, at the Mountain Gate Cafe and Dairy Treat.

16.1 Enter the town of Star Lake.

(The lake is on your right.) There are plenty of services in town, including Padgett's IGA grocery.

18.1 Along the watery lowlands and cattail marsh, make sure to watch for water birds and for hawks overhead.

21.4 A beautiful picnic area.

22.9 Turn right for a 5-mile round-trip detour to the New York State Ranger School at Wanakena.

This jog can easily be omitted if you are in a hurry to get back to your car, but it is a lovely road at the edge of magnificent wilderness. Along this route, follow signs to the Ranger School, generally bearing left, following Ranger School Road.

Sunset over Cranberry Lake

24.2 *Halfway to the Ranger School you'll pass the Pinecone Restaurant, owned by Paul Alford, who graduated from the Ranger School. Note the dock by the back door. Inside, one of the planet's great collection of baseball caps hangs from the ceiling.*

25.4 *The Ranger School at Wanakena, reputedly the oldest school of forest technology in the nation.*

This area was once the headquarters of the Rich Lumber Company, owned by a man named Herbert Rich—who was. He was because of the valuable timber on all sides. He had several mills here, including one devoted to making the handles for buggy whips—in its day as important an industry as, say, making steering wheels today. Mr. Rich eventually cut down most of what had drawn him here in the first place, and his company moved east to

Vermont. He was replaced as the major tenant by the Ranger School, a proud institution charged with producing the rangers who take care of the Adirondacks and the Empire State's other natural treasures: the Catskills, the wild parts of Long Island, the forests of the Finger Lakes, and the southern tier. Isolated and remote, the school is by all accounts a place of hard work, and most of its graduates are held in high esteem in the Adirondacks (though not of course by poachers and other outlaws). The school is set in a lovely spot, perfect for a picnic—ducks and swans will probably cruise in to see if you're inclined to share. You're looking across at real wilderness.

25.5 *Loop to the left at the end of the Ranger School beach, and head back out behind the buildings, dropping left below the tennis courts at 25.7 before rejoining the Ranger School Road at 25.8 and passing the Pinecone once more at 26.7 miles.*

27.0 *Turn right for the 1-mile trip back to NY 3.*

28.0 *Turn right onto NY 3, following the sign to Cranberry Lake.*

33.1 *Pass the entrance to Peavine Swamp trailhead, a wonderful place to walk or ski, though not offering grand vistas.*

35.0 *Cross the bridge by the Cranberry Lake boat launch where this tour began, continuing to the Mobil station at 35.1 miles.*

Just east of the end of this tour is the town of Cranberry Lake, which offers a number of small restaurants, hotels, and groceries. The most attractive store is definitely The Emporium, bulging with every kind of dry good, canned good, and T-shirt; it also has a marina. A good place to eat your food, and to stay the night or the week, is the state campground just east of town on the shore of the lake on Long Pine Road. More information is available by calling 315-848-2315, or you can reserve a campsite at 1-800-456-CAMP.

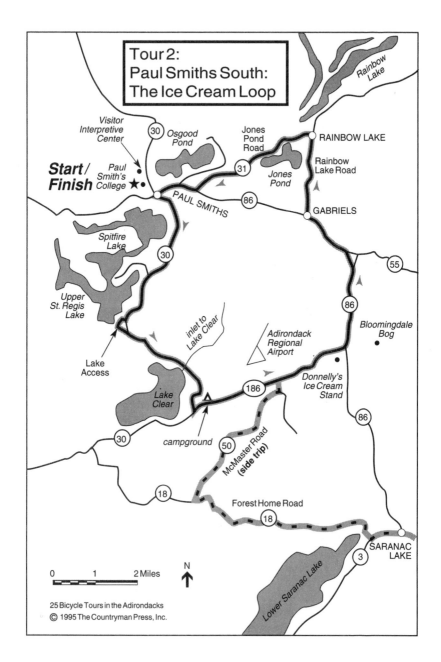

Tour 2:
Paul Smiths South:
The Ice Cream Loop

Visitor Interpretive Center

30 Osgood Pond

Jones Pond Road

RAINBOW LAKE

Rainbow Lake

Start / Finish

Paul Smith's College

31 Jones Pond

Rainbow Lake Road

PAUL SMITHS

86

GABRIELS

30 Spitfire Lake

55

Upper St. Regis Lake

86

Bloomingdale Bog

inlet to Lake Clear

Adirondack Regional Airport

Lake Access

186

Donnelly's Ice Cream Stand

86

Lake Clear

30

campground

50 McMaster Road (**side trip**)

18

Forest Home Road

18

SARANAC LAKE

3

0   1   2 Miles

N

Lower Saranac Lake

25 Bicycle Tours in the Adirondacks
© 1995 The Countryman Press, Inc.

22

2

Paul Smiths South: The Ice Cream Loop

Distance: 21.3 miles
Terrain: Fairly easy, with only a few difficult hills

This loop skirts the edge of the St. Regis Canoe Area on the one side, and offers a stunning glimpse of the state's fifth highest mountain from the other—in a short and easy trek it traverses many different Adirondack parks.

The common threads that unite these various parts of the region are tied up in the story of Paul Smith, who came to the North Country before the Civil War to open a hotel. He was a devoted innkeeper, and his wife, Lydia, was by all accounts a magnificent cook. Before long those traits, combined with a sagacious shrewdness, had turned Smith into one of the barons of the park, owning 10 lakes and tens of thousands of acres of land.

His legacy lives on in the school that bears his name—his whole name. Paul Smith's College is one of two institutions of higher learning in the entire Adirondacks. (The other, a 2-year community college, is nearby at Saranac Lake.) Paul Smith's College specializes in the two subjects that captivated Paul Smith the man—forestry and hotel management. Its courses in forestry center on extensive woodlands surrounding the school; the college has granted easements to the state on these woodlands, ensuring that they will never be developed. The hospitality program is run from an august brick institution, the Hotel Saranac, in downtown Saranac Lake. There, students learn to manage the hotel and the dining room. A high point of the week is a grand Wednesday night buffet, devoted each week to a different ethnic group and not to be missed.

In recent years this unique school has begun to transform itself into a true "College of the Adirondacks." It is in the process of expanding to a 4-year school, and increasingly its courses take account of the booming interest in ecotourism and the growing need for environmental professionals as well as timber managers. But with any luck its distinctive traits will never fade—its world-class snowshoe-racing program, for instance.

In any event, this tour traverses all of Paul Smith's worlds—the working forests, the magnificent vistas, the intimate lakes that made him rich. And it offers, at almost exactly the halfway point, a bit of hospitality that he would surely have enjoyed.

0.0 **Begin at Paul Smith's College, at the junction of NY 86 and NY 30.**

The Paul Smith's campus is friendly to visitors, offering access to the chain of lakes at the top of the St. Regis system; it also offers a bookstore and snack bar. (The small campus is also down the road from the Visitors Interpretive Center—see Tour 3 for more details.)

As you leave Paul Smiths, turn right on NY 30, on a gentle uphill. The road is nicely paved with a decent shoulder, curving through a pine forest lined with wildflowers and offering intermittent glimpses of water to the right.

2.5 **Spitfire Lake is visible to the right.**

3.6 **Turn right on an unmarked road.**

This offers access to wonderful Upper St. Regis Lake, which is about 0.5 mile down the road past a post office and summer store. When the state acquired the access, part of the deal was that it wouldn't erect signs, so there often aren't great crowds at the part of the lakeshore designated for public access. It sits cheek-by-jowl with the mooring for motorboats of residents, many of whom are famous. ("See that inflatable—that belongs to the fashion photographer Bruce Weber," our informant told us.) The best craft on this water, however, are the small number of "Idem" sailboats built specifically to race with its light air. One is in the museum at Blue Mountain Lake; the other surviving craft have all been returned here over the years, and ply its glassy surface with exquisite grace.

4.1 **Leaving the parking area, take the right fork. You will then return to NY 30.**

4.5 **Turn right on NY 30.**

5.5 *Crest a small rise. Lake Clear is visible to the right.*

A fashionable spot, Lake Clear has a guest roster that over the years included Albert Einstein. (The Lodge at Lake Clear is a very nice place to stay—518–891–1489.)

6.1 **Cross the inlet to Lake Clear.**

A tenth of a mile farther, at 6.2, there is an unmarked road offering public access to Lake Clear, including a beach.

7.2 *The long driveway to Charlie's Inn, which offers lodging and cheap good food.*

In winters past, Charlie's Inn has been the headquarters for the Alpo series sled-dog races, a weekend full of happy, lunging huskies and happy, lunging mushers. In the early 1990s the race was suspended for lack of sponsorship, but if you happen to be in the neighborhood during the winter make sure to ask if it has been renewed (518-891-9858).

7.5 *Turn left onto NY 186, which is somewhat busier than the route you have been traveling, and boasts a crummier shoulder to boot.*

9.1 *The Adirondack Regional Airport on the left has a snack bar. USAir offers limited daily service to and from this airport, and the flight from Albany is a special joy—no flight in the East can match it for intensity of wilderness, as you fly up the Hudson and over the High Peaks.*

9.5 *KBJ's Country Store, on the right.*

9.6 *McMaster Road, on the right, connects with Forest Home Road, offering fine biking as well as access to the lovely Lower Saranac Lake.*

11.4 *As you approach the intersection with NY 86, the world opens up, offering an utterly magnificent vista of the MacKenzie Range and Whiteface Mountain.*

(Whiteface is the one with the castle on top—see Tour 7 for details.) While soaking in the splendid view, you might miss the shack directly to the right. This would be a tragedy. Donnelly's Soft Ice Cream is to soft ice cream what the Adirondacks is to eastern wilderness—the apogee, the zenith, the ultimate. It is not like Howard Johnson's—there is one flavor each day, take it or leave it. Take it. The ice cream, made on site, is so rich and creamy that it tastes hardly sweetened. It is ice cream. You can feel your arteries hardening with each lick, but you have ridden 11 miles, and you have 10 more to go, and you might never pass this way again.

As you leave the parking lot at Donnelly's, turn left, returning to the intersection and continuing straight on NY 86, heading uphill.

The views to the right continue to be superb, and as you climb the hill you can more clearly see the Bloomingdale Bog beneath you. A lovely place, accessible along an old railroad bed, the bog is a wide expanse of sphagnum out of which grow cranberries, various orchids, and any number of other plants. The Nature Conservancy has protected some of the rarest portions, and the state owns much of the rest.

12.2 *A cemetery at the top of the hill offers a fine view and a good lunch spot; it also marks the start of a long descent, with Loon Mountain straight ahead as you drop through the farm fields.*

13.8 *The Asplind Christmas Tree Farm also houses an unusual gift shop, open year-round.*

14.5 *Climb again to the height-of-land. These are seed potatoes growing all around you, on the fertile glacial till that dominates the area.*

14.9 *Enter the town of Gabriels.*

15.2 *Ted's Grocery is on the right, and easy to miss as it is set back from the road a short distance.*

15.3 *Turn right on Rainbow Lake Road.*

15.4 *Pass a playground and ball field on the left.*

17.3 *Turn left on Jones Pond Road in the hamlet of Rainbow Lake.*
This is a very quiet and winding road—you're as likely to see the Paul Smiths snowshoe team out doing roadwork as you are to come across much traffic.

17.9 *Jones Pond is visible on the left, and the short canoe-carry to Rainbow Lake can be seen on the right.*

Donnelly's, the ice cream you earn

Jones Pond is the highest source of the east branch of the St. Regis River and is a pleasant place to swim.

18.4 *The wetlands at the head of Jones Pond are rich in beaver, heron, osprey, wood ducks, and other wildlife. Eagles are sighted here regularly.*

18.5 *Cross the outlet to the Osgood River, and notice the extension of the large Rainbow Lake esker, a narrow and well-defined ridge left by the glacier when it melted.*

20.2 *At Brighton Town Hall, turn right on NY 86.*

20.6 *A road to the right accesses Osgood Pond, the Paul Smith's collegiate sugarbush (the college is famed for its maple syrup), and the Northbrook Lodge, a former Adirondack great camp now converted to a lovely and quiet hostelry (518-327-3279).*

21.3 *Return to Paul Smiths.*

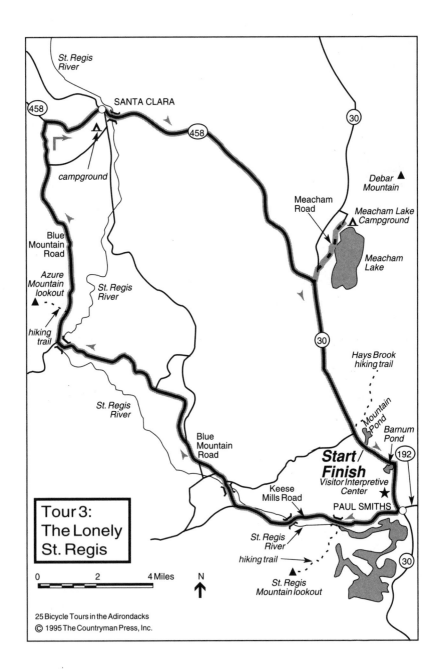

St. Regis
River

SANTA CLARA

458

458

campground

Debar
Mountain

30

Meacham
Road

Meacham Lake
Campground

Blue
Mountain
Road

Meacham
Lake

Azure
Mountain
lookout

St. Regis
River

hiking
trail

30

Hays Brook
hiking trail

St. Regis
River

Mountain
Pond

Barnum
Pond

Blue
Mountain
Road

192

**Start /
Finish**
Visitor Interpretive
Center

Keese
Mills Road

PAUL SMITHS

30

St. Regis
River

hiking trail

St. Regis
Mountain lookout

Tour 3:
The Lonely
St. Regis

0   2   4 Miles

N

25 Bicycle Tours in the Adirondacks
© 1995 The Countryman Press, Inc.

28

3
The Lonely St. Regis

Distance: *47.8 miles*
Terrain: *Difficult*

This loop begins and ends at the Visitors Interpretive Center in the town of Paul Smiths. The center, and its twin in the central Adirondack town of Newcomb, are recent additions to the park, lavish and beautiful attempts to bring tourists into hitherto isolated sections of the Adirondacks.

In the case of this facility, anyway, the attempt has succeeded. Drawn by a wide variety of exhibits, tourists have streamed in, and at least a few have abandoned their cars to explore the charms of the St. Regis Canoe Area and the Debar Mountain Wild Forest.

Almost no one, however, ventures down the dirt road that is at the heart of this ride. It wanders through the lowlands of the St. Regis River, land that is not, for the most part, state owned. Much of the land belongs to logging companies—Champion International has a facility in Santa Clara, once home to the mighty Santa Clara Lumber Company. You will also notice gated roads leading to large private estates of the sort that once dominated much of the park.

This river valley, and the forest along the paved but little-traveled return roads, is wild country. The river feels boreal, Canadian—boggy openings, sandy scrub. Along the paved return there is the illusion of being up quite high, an almost Western high. You will certainly see deer, owl, and other wildlife—it is also this part of the Adirondacks that produces the most consistent mountain lion sightings, as well as occasional tales of wolves. The state's Department of Environmental Conservation refuses to recognize the presence of either animal—but it is easy to imagine, in these empty miles, that almost anything might be living here.

Don't bother with this loop if you have a gentle day's outing in mind, or if you don't know how to change your tires—cars can be few and far between along the dirt stretch, and even on the paved road there are no services. But if it's isolation that draws you, a desire to feel small against the vast scale of the woods, this is the perfect trip to occupy soul and muscle for an entire day.

0.0 Visitors Interpretive Center, NY 30, Paul Smiths, NY.

A vast parking area makes this a natural spot from which to launch the tour, but its charms go much further. A series of nature trails, which offer excellent cross-country skiing in the winter, provide glimpses of almost every Adirondack habitat. In the large log building, films and exhibits introduce visitors to the park, and interactive computer screens provide advice on hiking, dining, and lodging. In the summer, a screened "butterfly house" lets you walk in and among hundreds of different butterflies and moths. On a more prosaic note, the VIC is a perfect place to empty bladders and fill water bottles.

Adirondack Visitors Interpretive Center, Paul Smiths

Once you're ready to go, turn right on NY 30 out the main exit.

0.8 *Turn right onto Keese Mills Road, just before the main entrance to Paul Smith's College.*

1.2 *On the left is the barn and equipment used by Paul Smith's students learning to log with horses.*

1.5 *A campground reserved for Paul Smith's alumni.*

2.8 *You'll begin to notice water on the left: a wetland and then a small pond at 3.0, with a pulloff. These waters are the source of the St. Regis River.*

3.3 *A river access at St. Regis Presbyterian Church (a summers-only congregation).*

3.4 *At the bridge you'll find signs to the trailhead for the climb to St. Regis Mountain.*

This is a round-trip hike of about 5 miles that offers the attraction of a fire tower with splendid views of the lakes and low mountains in the area, the High Peaks in the distance, and the river valley where you'll be spending most of the rest of the day. You are also near Camp Topridge, once the home of prominent socialite (and breakfast-cereal heiress) Marjorie Post.

4.4 *The pavement changes as you officially enter the town of Santa Clara.*

As is often the case in the Adirondacks, this township is enormous—the actual hamlet of Santa Clara is several hours' ride away. The road is on good pavement still, and winds beautifully through low woods, marshes, and fields returning to brush.

7.2 *Stay with the road as it swings to the right. The road name changes to Blue Mountain Road. (Straight ahead is Bay Pond, a Rockefeller estate.)*

8.3 *Cross a steel-deck bridge.*

9.1 *The road turns to dirt and gravel. Keep on the main track.*

Caution: Though the road is nice and wide, watch out for the potholes and puddles that have been filled with gravel and tend to be softer than the rest of the surface. Be especially careful on downhills at 10.2 and 12.1 miles, which tend to be a little sandy. The terrain turns ever more boreal, offering tantalizing glimpses of open lowlands through the trees.

16.1 *A steep uphill section, one of the very few on this dirt section of the tour. It is followed by a downhill that was a little washed out in 1994.*

17.8 *The first house in a long stretch, right at a bridge that offers a wonderful view of the now-roaring St. Regis in a stretch of white water.*

19.2 *The trail to Azure Mountain, one of the few state properties in the area.*

(Though conservationists have long dreamed of adding this boreal wildland to the state's protected areas, the drive seems largely to have stalled in recent years.) The quick climb—2 hours, round trip—takes you to an abandoned fire tower, on a mountain with wonderful cliffs where state wildlife officials have released young falcons to the wild in recent years. This may be the best view there is of the taiga through which you have been riding—a truly wild place.

23.8 *Pavement! It's always amazing how smooth the road feels after a good long stretch of bumpy dirt. You can thank the Blue Mountain Paving Company, which is located directly to your left, the first business passed so far on this trip.*

26.2 *Come to a stop sign, and turn right on NY 458, part of the old military road that ran from the Champlain to the St. Lawrence Valley and was crucial in the War of 1812.*

28.7 *This is Santa Clara!*

White's Santa Clara Lodge is the only business in town.

29.0 *A road right leads to the Santa Clara campground.*

29.1 *A bridge crosses the St. Regis River, offering a good view. The Champion sign identifies the lumber company now dominant in this area.*

29.9 *One of the stiffer ascents on this tour begins, taking you up to the high ground. This road boasts a great shoulder, happily, though traffic is usually scarce.*

33.2 *A parking turnout and picnic area on the right.*

37.4 *Another parking turnout, this one with a marker explaining the importance of forest fires in creating the current landscape.*

39.6 *Turn right on NY 30, following signs to Saranac Lake and Tupper Lake.*

(Turning left will bring you fairly quickly to the public campground at Meacham Lake, a 1200-acre lake.) This road is somewhat busier than NY 458, at least on summer weekends, and the shoulder is not uniformly as good.

39.8 *The Meacham Lake General Store, which as of 1994 was empty, with only a sign offering it for rent at reasonable rates. Someone should fill the vacancy, if only to make this tour more hospitable.*

45.0 *After winding past small ponds and through deeper woods, the road passes the Hays Brook trailhead, a major access point to the Debar Mountain Wild Forest (the other is at Meacham Lake).*

This area, officially designated for horse trails, is used by many mountain bikers—hiking maven Barbara McMartin recommends the trip to the Sheep Meadow, a distance of 3.6 miles.

46.1 *The road to Mountain Pond is passed on the left. It is an easy ride down, and the reward is a place to swim or fish.*

46.6 *Barnum Pond appears on the right, offering additional swimming opportunities. A trail from the Visitors Interpretive Center runs to this pond, and skirts its edge on a boardwalk.*

47.8 *Reach the Visitors Interpretive Center once more. A large wooden deck at the back of the center is perfect for relaxing after the rigors of this lonely, beautiful ride.*

4

St. Regis: Into the Woods

Distance: *41.4 miles*
Terrain: *Moderate*

The town of St. Regis Falls, where this tour begins, is located in the northern reaches of the Adirondack Park, less than 20 miles below the Canadian border. The town itself—a typical North Country outpost—is not as old as surrounding hamlets; it was founded in 1880 during the logging boom, and swelled rapidly to more than 2000 inhabitants by the turn of the century. Today just under a thousand people live here. There is a school, a store, a post office, a church—and not a lot more.

The town's highlight is the St. Regis Falls Scenic Campground, located at the falls below the dam on the St. Regis River. The campground was built in 1966, during President Johnson's Great Society program, and is a beautiful setting for an overnight stay or a picnic. Tent or trailer sites are available on the edge of the river, as well as eight log cabins overlooking the falls. Fishing in the river, near the falls, yields northern pike, bass, and bullhead. For information or reservations, call 518-856-9277.

The tour begins at the intersections of County Routes 5 and 14; a United Methodist Church and the St. Regis Central School are at the corner.

0.0 *Begin riding east on County Road 14; this is Red Tavern Road.*

2.2 *As you pass the marshes, you might see a woodchuck or two running through a yard into the reeds.*

2.6 *At Trim Hill Road, veer left to stay on County Road 14.*

As you leave town, the road narrows, but this is not a concern, as there is little traffic. Wildflowers and ferns line the road, leading into deciduous woods. At times, the treetops meet across the road; the effect is most pleasing, rather like gliding along a forest path.

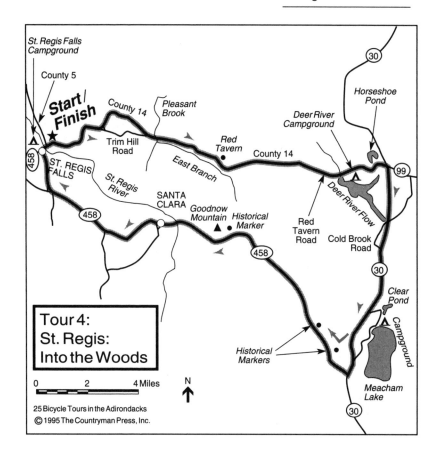

Tour 4:
St. Regis:
Into the Woods

0   2   4 Miles

N

25 Bicycle Tours in the Adirondacks
© 1995 The Countryman Press, Inc.

5.3 *Cross Pleasant Brook, which flows into the East Branch.*
County Road 14 follows the East Branch, offering some
delightful views of the water on your right.

9.1 *Note the Red Tavern on the left.*

This was the first hotel in the area, built in the late 1850s, long before the town of St. Regis Falls existed. It was a stagecoach stop on
the Fort Kent Road for many years.

10.2 *Begin a 0.5-mile easy uphill climb. Note the profusion of*
black-eyed Susans, Queen Anne's lace, trillium, and ferns along
the road.

13.0 *Cross the Deer River Flow.*

St. Regis Falls, from the campground

13.7 The Deer River Campground is on your right.

14.7 Cross over Horseshoe Pond Run.

15.2 Turn right (south) onto NY 30.

NY 30 is also known as the Adirondack Trail because it cuts north–south through the entire Adirondack Park. The road is wider here, with good shoulders, and somewhat more traffic. Pines begin to replace the deciduous woods of the Red Tavern Road.

17.5 At the intersection of Cold Brook Road, note the open water, which is the end of the Deer River Flow, to the right.

19.0 Begin a gentle, 2-mile climb.

20.6 The water to the left is Clear Pond.

20.9 The access road to the Meacham Lake Campground and Day-Use Area turns off to the left; the campground is approximately 1 mile from NY 30. Begin a gradual descent for the next couple miles.

23.6 Cross the Meacham Lake Flow.

23.8 *Turn right (west) onto NY 458.*

Again, there is a nice shoulder on this route and an easy downhill grade.

24.5 *The historical marker on the right marks the location of the old Northwest Bay Road, which was begun in 1810. The intention was to link Lake Champlain in the east with the St. Lawrence River in the west, but the road only extended to Hopkinton, about 5 miles west of St. Regis Falls.*

24.8 *Begin a gentle climb through more wooded country.*

25.8 *The historical marker on the right recalls the forest fire of May 1903, which burned 10,000 acres of woods in this area.*

25.9 *At the top of the hill, the woods give way to a marsh.*

27.7 *Begin to climb again.*

28.2 *This spot marks the location of Jenning Road, which was used by US troops during the War of 1812 as they marched west from Lake Champlain to Lake Ontario. You can just make out the road, which is now a grassy opening in the woods.*

32.8 *Reach the height-of-land (1815 feet) as you cross over the flank of Goodnow Mountain. Enjoy a long descent on the other side.*

34.2 *As you cross the St. Regis River, herons can often be seen in the water near the bridge.*

The town of Santa Clara is just on the other side of the river, with a climb up out of town. The next 5 miles are rolling, with a couple of short, fairly steep climbs.

39.8 *Your hill-climbing is rewarded with a broad view of the St. Lawrence valley stretching away to the northwest into Canada. Begin a descent into St. Regis Falls.*

As you come into town, notice the sign for the "Adirondack Laundromat and Carwash."

41.2 *Cross the St. Regis River one more time, just below the dam.*

To the left is Gigi's Grocery, and just past the grocery is the St. Regis Falls Scenic Campground. Continue straight to return to your starting point.

41.4 *Return again to the intersection of Red Tavern Road.*

5

Norman Ridge and Environs: The Big View

Distance: *29.8 miles*
Terrain: *Moderately difficult, with a number of ups and downs*

This tour is perhaps the most Vermontlike of any in this book, and hence one of the most popular. It offers several long stretches of open farm and meadow, which come as a welcome shock to anyone who has spent days cycling through the mostly closed-in woods of the Adirondacks.

It's not that people didn't try to farm the Adirondacks. Hikers know quite well that they did—miles from nowhere, in what seem like virgin woods to untrained eyes, they'll often stumble across a stone wall or an old cellarhole, a stand of apple trees now gone to wild or an old and rambling lilac bush that once perfumed a now-vanished kitchen window. (We even found an old hop vine once, and brewed beer flavored with its pungent flowers.) But anyone who has tried to grow an Adirondack garden realizes why there are so few farms left today—it's not safe to put plants into the ground before Memorial Day, and even then people save a few tomatoes inside to replant in case of a late frost; the first frost of the new fall often comes in late August.

Add that climate—maybe 5 percent harsher than New England's—to the inherent difficulties of transporting crops from this mountainous and remote terrain and you can understand why—outside the Champlain Valley where the water moderates winter's blast—there is little agriculture left in the park. And as soon as the plowing and haying stopped, the forests began to fill back in—it surprises people how fast the woods will reclaim a field, but there are plenty of Adirondackers who grew up in farming towns where not a pasture remains. "If it weren't for the lawnmower, there wouldn't be no grass here at all," one old-timer once complained to us.

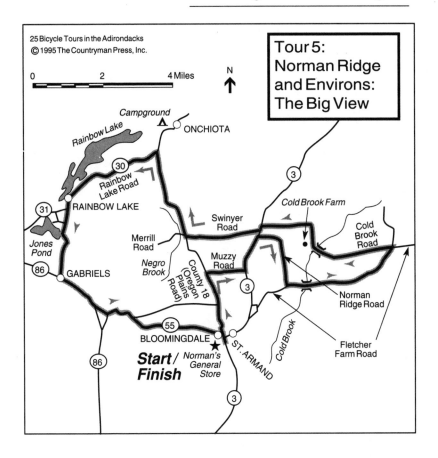

But that's what makes this trip such a delightful exception. The glacial silt and high sand along the high plateau on Norman Ridge and NY 86 make them exceptional locations for raising high-quality seed potatoes; the open fields feel bald and exposed, perched under the massive mountains. You feel like Julie Andrews in the Alps.

0.0 *Begin at Norman's General Store in the heart of Bloomingdale, a small community north of Saranac Lake. Stand facing the entrance of Norman's, and then ride to the left of the store, down County Road 18 (Oregon Plains Road).*

0.1 *At an unmarked fork by an abandoned church, bear right.*

Training the next generation on Oregon Plains Road

0.2   *Turn right in front of the Steakside restaurant.*

0.3   *Cross the brook and bear left on Oregon Plains Road.*

1.6   *Begin a long, gentle climb up this pine-lined stretch of road, occasionally glancing back over your shoulder to see the mountains emerging into view.*

2.0   *As the hill tops out, turn right on Muzzy Road—but not before pausing for one more backward glance at the McKenzie Range.*

3.2   *Turn left onto NY 3, a more heavily traveled road but with a wide shoulder.*

3.9   *Pass a small country store on your left.*

4.2   *Turn right on Norman Ridge Road, and immediately begin a moderate uphill grade.*

4.8 As you crest the hill, a stunning view awaits you. From left to right, you're looking at Marble Mountain, Whiteface (the tallest peak, and the one with the castle on top), and the McKenzie Range. These beautiful open fields will, one hopes, remain free from development, despite the attractions of their beautiful views—as you ride, repeat to yourself: "I will not build a summer house here."

5.0 As you round a slight bend, the High Peaks come into view— Nippletop is especially prominent, as are the Sawtooths. The only structures up here are some gray and aging barns, and they only add to the beauty of the scene.

5.6 Begin a long and fairly steep downhill.

6.2 Turn left on Fletcher Farm Road.

6.6 As you pass a house on the right, notice the strange barrel-shaped little hut near the road. This is the headquarters of the Adirondack's foremost sauna company, producing the elegant little structures that win raves from the cognoscenti of heat.

6.8 Cross a steel-deck bridge.

8.0 The views open up again to the right, and there are particularly fine glimpses of Whiteface, with a view of the ornate structure on top of the mountain, usually crowded with tourists who have driven up the toll road to the top.

9.7 Left on Cold Brook Farm Road.

10.5 Now the view opens dramatically to the west, with St. Regis Mountain prominent.

12.0 Begin a series of uphills, which, though not steep, feel fairly stiff at this stage of the tour.

12.6 Cross Cold Brook, past Cold Brook Farm, whose proprietors offer visitors the chance to fish in their pond. (Year-round, in case you'd like to come back and try a little ice fishing.) You don't need a license.

14.1 Return to NY 3. A couple of hundred yards to the right another small country store is visible, but unless you are going there *to reprovision, turn left and go about 50 yards down NY 3 before turning right at the first opportunity, on Swinyer Road.*

16.4 Go right on Oregon Plains Road. (Across this intersection is a dirt road, Merrill Road, which will cross Negro Brook before reaching the old railroad grade that bisects the Bloomingdale Bog, and which offers fascinating biking north or south.)

19.1 Turn left on Rainbow Lake Road. (If you are looking for camping, the Buck Pond Campground is nearby to the right in Onchiota. It offers swimming, showers, and canoe or rowboat rental; call 518-891-3449.)

21.6 Enter the hamlet of Rainbow Lake.

21.8 Cross a power line right-of-way that offers access right or left.

22.4 Pass Jones Pond Road to the right, with public access to swimming.

24.3 Playground and picnic tables on the right provide a good spot for lunch.

24.4 Turn left onto NY 86.

24.5 Pass Ted's General Store on the left.

25.0 Crest the hill, with more mountain views.

25.7 Bear left onto County Road 55, following signs to Bloomingdale.

26.1 Bear left around the corner.

29.1 Enter the town of Bloomingdale.

29.7 Connect the loop, with the old church on your left. Continue straight ahead.

29.8 Back to Norman's General Store, and the Four Corners diner located directly across the street.

6
Dannemora: The Iron Range

Distance: *38.6 miles (adding an optional 24.6-mile loop in the middle makes this a 63.2-mile route)*
Terrain: *Difficult, with several long, serious climbs (the optional loop is easy and mostly flat)*

Up in the northern reaches of the Adirondack Park, just 20 miles south of the Canadian border, the last mountains of the Adirondacks give way to the more level fields of the St. Lawrence valley. The towns of Dannemora and Lyon Mountain lie at the junction of mountain and valley, with the High Peaks just to the south.

This area was settled around its iron mines, and at one time many boomtowns thrived along this route; today, most of the communities are small, many are dying, and a few have vanished altogether. In Lyon Mountain, you can still see the remains of the mining buildings, and enormous piles of tailings, the impurities left from refining the iron.

The route begins in the town of Dannemora, nestled at the foot of Dannemora and Johnson Mountains. Dannemora is the site of the Clinton State Correctional Facility, which is located in, and overwhelms, the center of town. In fact, as you travel down Main Street, the prison's 20-foot walls, guard towers, and razor wire loom above you. The effect is rather subduing.

The prison dates back to 1845, when inmates were transferred from Auburn State and Sing Sing Prisons to work the iron deposits in Dannemora Mountain. After a couple of brutally cold, windy winters, Clinton Prison became known as the "Siberia of the North." Once mining declined, the prison set up other, lighter industries within its walls, as well as educational and arts courses, and it is rumored that a ski jump exists within the prison complex.

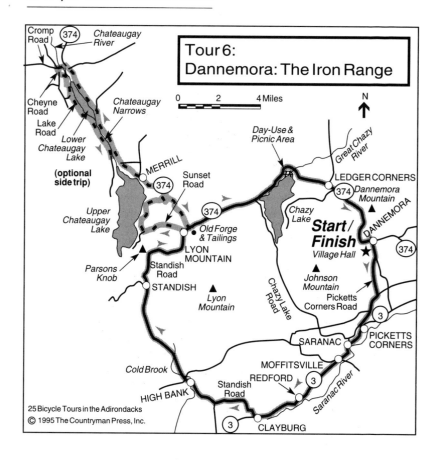

Tour 6:
Dannemora: The Iron Range

Dannemora has a small but well-equipped bike shop, located at the corner of Cook Street and General Leroy Manor Road. Steve Coulton, the owner of the aptly named Steve's Bike Shop, is more than willing to do emergency repairs, offer tips on riding in the area, and just chat about the town. There are several diners and small motels in town as well.

This route begins at the Dannemora Village Hall, just south of the main drag on Emmons Street. You can park your car there and use the bathrooms if the hall is open.

0.0   Turn right out of the village hall parking lot, riding south on Emmons Street.

As you ride, you will descend through farmland into the Saranac

River valley. The High Peaks rise majestically on the other side. There's not much shoulder, but traffic is not very heavy.

0.6 *Joining NY 374, the road bears to the right, still descending gradually.*

4.2 *Here, in the hamlet of Picketts Corners, turn right onto NY 3.*

There is more shoulder here that compensates for the higher volume of traffic. You'll soon pass Bud's Diner, an unassuming place that serves fantastic food at great prices. A Citgo minimart offers much less exciting fare.

5.6 *Note the Saranac River on your left, which you will follow for the next 6 miles. It flows northeast into Lake Champlain at Plattsburgh.*

5.9 *Enter the hamlet of Saranac, not to be confused with Saranac Lake, which lies some 35 miles to the southwest.*

6.4 *Cross True Brook as you enter the small hamlet of Moffitsville.*

6.7 *Begin a gradual but steady 1-mile climb out of Moffitsville.*

8.7 *Enter the hamlet of Redford.*

10.0 *Just past Redford, a parking area on the left offers a great view of the river, and a nice place to stop for a moment.*

11.2 *Enter the town of Clayburg.*

The Clayburg Grocery stocks most anything you'll need, and it's the last place you'll be able to fill your water bottles until Lyon Mountain, 15 miles away.

11.7 *Turn right onto Standish Road.*

The road is narrow, without any kind of shoulder, but traffic is virtually nonexistent. Just after the turn, you'll begin a steady climb for 2 miles. At the top, a view of the High Peaks rewards your hard work.

13.7 *A long downhill awaits you—enjoy!*

15.4 *You'll cross Cold Brook several times in the next mile or so.*

16.2 *Just about all that remains of the hamlet of High Bank, once a mining village, is the four-corner intersection and a few houses. You'll climb again as you leave town, up and over the flank of Lyon Mountain.*

19.4 *At the height-of-land, you'll begin a long, well-deserved descent.*

21.5 *Enter the hamlet of Standish, also little more than a collection of a few homes and stone row houses.*

Here, in 1881, the Catalan Forge Furnace refined iron from the Saranac River mines. Only 5 years later, in 1886, it was replaced by a larger furnace in the town of Lyon Mountain, to the north.

21.9 *Turn right onto Standish Road, which may not be marked.*

23.5 *The Upper Chateaugay Lake is visible to your left, on the other side of Parson's Knob Hill.*

23.9 *On your left, note the Parson's Mine Shaft Restaurant and Store, an effort to bring tourism to the remains of the mining industry.*

24.5 *A spring on the side of the road offers good, cold water for your bottles.*

25.4 *You'll know you're entering the hamlet of Lyon Mountain by the rows of houses originally built for the miners and their families.*

25.7 *The Lyon Mountain Railroad Station is on your right.*

Just behind the station, up the side of Lyon Mountain, are the remains of the Lyon Mountain Forge Furnace. Enormous piles of tailings ring the forge buildings. Today, Lyon Mountain offers services to a seasonal community on the Upper Chateaugay Lake.

26.0 *Note the Mobil station on your left. To continue to Dannemora, bear right onto NY 374.*

Optional Lower Chateaugay Lake Loop

At this point, if you wish to add a fairly easy 25 miles to your ride, you may take a scenic loop around the Lower Chateaugay Lake to the northwest. This long, narrow lake, dammed at its outlet, lies in the valley of Figure Eight Mountain and Spruce and Panther Hills.

0.0 *Just past the Lyon Mountain Railroad Station, turn left onto Sunset Road, which leads downhill to the Upper Chateaugay Lake.*

2.4 Bear right at the fork; the lake will be in view from time to time on the left as you ride.

4.8 Turn left onto NY 374, which offers a good shoulder for riding.

5.6 You may have thought you left the rat race behind, but J.L.'s Express Lane Deli preserves the fast life, if only in its name.

6.2 Enter the town of Merrill, which offers views of the lake to the left.

7.8 The Hollywood Restaurant is near the boat launch.

8.2 Pass Narrows Road on your left, which crosses the Chateaugay Narrows, a 3-mile stretch of water connecting the Upper and Lower Chateaugay Lakes. Vacation and year-round homes line the water, with catchy names like "Smith's Narrow Escape."

10.4 Bear left at the fork, staying on NY 374, as you enter Franklin County.

12.4 The Knotty Pine Restaurant offers good, basic food.

13.3 Turn left onto Cromp Road, where you'll cross the Chateaugay River. This was the location of the largest Catalan Forge in the world, which operated from 1871 to 1883.

14.0 Turn left on Cheyne Road. You'll be traveling down the other side of the lake.

14.1 Immediately turn left on Lake Road, a small road that runs close to the water. It rolls up and down a fair amount, in small hills. Once again, the water is lined with many summer and year-round dwellings.

17.3 The road turns to dirt, but only for 0.4 mile.

19.0 At the stop sign, turn left onto Narrows Road, crossing the Chateaugay Narrows.

19.1 Turn right onto NY 374 to head back to Lyon Mountain.

22.6 You'll pass Sunset Road on the right, but continue straight on NY 374.

As you come down the hill into Lyon Mountain, you'll have a good view of the old forge and tailings.

24.2 Enter the hamlet of Lyon Mountain.

24.6 Pass the Mobil station on your left.

Rejoin the original route to Dannemora.

26.0 At the Mobil station, bear right onto NY 374.

The shoulder is fairly wide, but not always in good condition. You'll begin to climb for about 2 miles.

28.2 At the top of the hill, as you catch your breath, you can see Chazy Lake in the distance. Now the road descends.

29.7 Chazy Lake Road, on your right, leads back to the town of Saranac.

30.4 Noel's Grocery carries the basics. Pick up lunch supplies, if you need them, and carry them with you to the day-use area, I mile ahead.

31.6 The Chazy Lake Day-Use and Picnic Area is a good place for a rest, a snack, and a swim.

32.1 You'll often see folks fishing from the dam across the Great Chazy River.

32.4 After the beach on your right, you'll leave Chazy Lake.

Here the countryside opens up to farms, reaching north into the St. Lawrence Valley.

34.5 Pass the Ledger Corners General Store. Stay on NY 374.

34.7 Begin the last and most serious climb of the route, over the pass between Dannemora and Johnson Mountains.

36.9 At the top of the pass, you'll find a spring with good water on your right. Looking ahead, you'll be treated to a magnificent view of the Adirondack High Peaks, with Vermont's Green Mountains to your left.

Enjoy the view while you're at the top of the hill, because you're about to begin a 2-mile-long, steep descent. You've earned it! But you'll be paying too much attention to the road to catch the view around you.

38.6 The downhill brings you back into the hamlet of Dannemora. Turn right onto Emmons Street to return to the village hall.

7

Saranac, Placid, and Whiteface: Up, Down, and Through the Towns

Distance: *46 miles*
Terrain: *Difficult, with one sustained climb and the traffic of Lake Placid to dodge*

You will be riding through all kinds of history along this classic ride, first suggested to us by Jim Tucker. In the city of Saranac Lake, for instance, you will pass by the rows of "cure cottages" where tuberculosis sufferers flocked in the late 19th century to take the mountain air and recover. (The Trudeau family, descendants of the founding doctor, are still in residence, and the institute they have built continues to do pathbreaking research on TB and other diseases. Garry Trudeau, the creator of the "Doonesbury" comic strip, is the most famous member of the current generation, and a native of the town.)

A little farther down the road, the town of Lake Placid is crammed with athletic history. The only town in North America to have hosted two Winter Olympics (in 1932 and 1980), the town prospered from its identification with ice and snow. Now it is crowded year-round—the most famous spot in the park, it draws hordes of visitors, as well as throngs of athletes training at the Olympic Training Center and using the various official Olympic venues. (And not just in winter—the ski jumps, for instance, are covered with a plastic that allows summer leaps.) Most of the Olympic sites are open year-round, and in winter you can really sense the history by plummeting down the bobsled run yourself.

Farther still along this ride you will pass the Whiteface Mountain Ski Center, where the skiing events were held for the Olympics, and where wintertime visitors find the highest vertical drop in the Northeast: 3216 feet. Whiteface itself, at 4867 feet the state's fifth highest peak, is unique

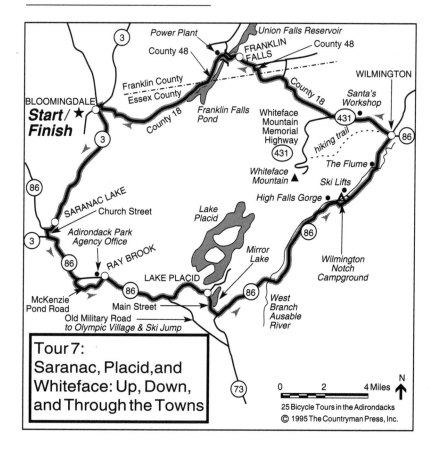

Tour 7:
Saranac, Placid, and
Whiteface: Up, Down,
and Through the Towns

25 Bicycle Tours in the Adirondacks
© 1995 The Countryman Press, Inc.

among the tall peaks of the Adirondacks, both for the toll road that brings visitors to its summit (it is, thankfully, closed to cyclists so you will not be tempted by the climb) and for the atmospheric research station on its slopes, which is charting the new and perhaps more depressing history of the Adirondacks: acid rain, ozone pollution, global warming.

All in all, this is one of the most interesting rides in this book. It has stretches of great quiet and beauty, but there are plenty of reminders of the past, present, and future impact of people on these mountains.

0.0   *Begin at the Four Corners in Bloomingdale.*

(You can pick up this loop, of course, at any point, and many may choose to begin in Lake Placid. But the Bloomingdale start and finish allows you to get through the most urban section of the ride fairly early on and to end with a lovely and refreshing jaunt past water and woods.)

From the Four Corners (where Norman's General Store offers a chance to provision, and the Four Corners Diner an opportunity to eat) head south on NY 3 toward Saranac Lake, passing a cemetery at 1.2 miles, a quarry at 2.5 miles, and a boatworks at 3.6 miles.

4.5 *A small bog here is particularly beautiful in early fall, when the swamp maples turn first, their bright scarlet leaves framing the water.*

5.8 *Enter the town of Saranac Lake.*

6.6 *Turn left on Church Street, past the Grand Union, and then up a rise.*

As you pedal down Church Street, you will see signs pointing out the Robert Louis Stevenson cottage to the left. Like so many others (Jack Dempsey, Legs Diamond) he came here to take the cure, and while he was here in 1887–1888 he wrote extensively. The house is now open to the public during the summer.

7.0 *Turn left (very carefully) onto NY 86. The body of water is Lake Flower; it is at this spot, during the annual winter carnival, that a great palace of ice is constructed each year, and lit to gleam at night.*

7.3 *When NY 86 bears right, you get off it by continuing straight.*

Caution: This is a tricky intersection to negotiate. Definitely walk your bike. Head down McKenzie Pond Road past the Pendragon Theater and disappear into lovely rolling woods.

10.1 *Turn left onto NY 86 again in the town of Ray Brook.*

You are at the administrative center of the park.

Not only is there a State Police office, and the regional center of the Department of Environmental Conservation, there is also the office of the Adirondack Park Agency. Though reviled by many in the park as an infringement on property rights, the APA's administration of zoning codes has helped protect the open character of the Adirondacks. They have no jurisdiction over city centers, however, and you will soon see the results of unregulated growth as you approach Lake Placid. For the moment, be careful—NY 86 is a busy, narrow-shouldered road, perhaps the most-traveled section of pavement in the park. People turn on and off constantly, attracted by enterprises like the Smokehouse BBQ (at 10.6 miles), which is well worth a stop.

11.6 *The road passes through a section of research forest, which has been planted to plantation pine—notice the straight rows, and how they differ from the diverse and real forests you have encountered on this tour and many others in this book.*

12.3 *An uphill stretch.*

13.3 *Stay on NY 86, as it passes the intersection with Old Military Road.*

(If you have time you might want to take this spur—it offers access to several Olympic venues as well as the farm of famed abolitionist John Brown and the northern terminus of the Northville–Lake Placid Trail.)

14.2 *As you enter the town of Lake Placid, you will see a sudden and remarkable increase in schlock. Many Adirondackers refer to this community as Lake Plastic. There are shopping malls and franchise restaurants ahead—and perhaps a Walmart. As this book went to press, an enormous battle was raging in town over the giant retailer's plans to construct a new outlet.*

15.6 *A steep downhill will take you to the center of town. Turn right at the bottom, and ride along Main Street.*

(A left will take you to the charming Mirror Lake Inn.) The town, besides its outlet stores, has several spots of interest to bicyclists—Eastern Mountain Sports, on the left in the center of town, is one. A few doors down, at With Pipe and Book, you will find an excellent selection of Adirondack books, as well as the region's best-stocked humidor. To your left is Mirror Lake, a lovely body of water summer or winter. You can rent a canoe at Jones Outfitters near EMS.

16.0 *After the Winter Sports Museum, the road climbs steeply to*

the Olympic Center at 16.2, and Lake Placid High School at 16.3.

Directly in front of the high school is the speed-skating rink where Eric Heiden garnered five gold medals in 1980.

16.5 *Go straight through the stoplight.*

16.6 *Straight ahead through this stoplight, too, following signs to Whiteface Mountain.*

Within 0.2 mile you will hit a golf course, and you will be out of town, away from many of the cars and all of the shops. The pavement turns smoother, the grade drops gently, life is good.

19.8 *You'll cross a bridge over the West Branch of the Ausable, and probably see a few fly-fishermen.*

From now on you'll have this gorgeous river on your left for a long stretch, passing small falls and parking turnouts every few tenths of a mile. The road is busy, twisting, and narrow; the shoulder is definitely better heading in this direction. Dismount occasionally, and cross the road to look at or explore the river—it is well worth the trip.

24.4 *High Falls Gorge, a commercial enterprise, charges admission to see their chain of waterfalls. The road pulls away from the river for a little while.*

25.4 *The Wilmington Notch Campgrounds and Day-Use Area provides access to the Ausable.*

25.7 *You will cross the entrance to Whiteface Mountain, the premier downhill ski mountain in the Adirondacks.*

26.8 *As you pass the Hungry Trout restaurant (which in fact serves trout to hungry people) you will have views of both Whiteface Mountain and the foaming rapids of the Flume.*

27.8 *A store offers camping supplies as you come into Wilmington. Farther along you'll pass a pancake house and an A&W Rootbeer stand.*

28.9 *Turn left at the intersection, following NY 431 and the signs to Whiteface Mountain Memorial Highway.*

(A convenience store at this corner is the last place to reprovision on this trip.) As soon as you have made the turn, you will begin to climb, a steady ascent that lasts more than 3.5 miles. It is never horribly steep, but it is unrelenting, and the pavement is lousy, especially at first. It may take you 40 minutes or more to make the climb, and you will likely be in your lowest gear most of the way.

29.5 *Pass Reservoir Road on the left, which offers access to the trailhead for hikers heading up Whiteface.*

30.6 *Santa's Workshop is on the right, a slightly down-at-the-heels tourist attraction. There is a small locomotive engine out front—just keep repeating to yourself "I think I can, I think I can."*

31.0 *A sign informs you that you are a mile from the tollbooth on Whiteface, and hence a mile away from the end of the steepest part of the climb. A little farther on the pavement improves. To the left you'll see the entrance to the Atmospheric Research Center, where important work on environmental contamination is under way.*

31.8 *Just before reaching the tollbooth, bear right onto County Road 18, following the signs to Franklin Falls and Bloomingdale.*

There is a fishing hole here, but it is only for the use of children and the handicapped.

32.5 *The trailhead for Cooper Kiln Road marks the height-of-land. Soon you will start downhill.*

Caution: If the climb was long and strenuous, the descent is long and dangerous. The pavement is bad, the road twists constantly, and there is no shoulder at all, just a sandy strip that will flip you in an instant. Do not let yourself get going too fast.

33.7 *As you enter the boundary of St. Armand, the road flattens a bit, and then turns steep and twisty once more. (The town of St. Armand, by the way, does not exist. St. Armand is, rather, a vast township comprising several hamlets and villages.)*

35.0 *Keep on the main road, following the Franklin Falls sign. You will wind downhill to a steel-deck bridge, and then the road flattens out in fields.*

36.8 A sharp left and then steeply downhill. The water you see at the bottom is the tail end of Union Falls Reservoir. You continue to the left.

38.2 The Niagara Mohawk power plant at Franklin Falls.

38.4 Cross the bridge and then turn left toward Bloomingdale.

There is a little turnout here, which offers a commanding view of Franklin Falls Reservoir, a dammed stretch of the Saranac River. From this point on, the road will follow the water, offering views and access to the left throughout. This is a lonely road; as this book went to press, much of it was under construction, so the pavement should be fresh and smooth.

45.8 Turn left on to NY 3.

46.0 Return to Bloomingdale.

Bike Shops

Barkeater Bicycle
45 Main St., Saranac Lake
full repair shop

High Peaks Cyclery
331 Main St., Lake Placid
full repair shop

Placid Planet
200 Saranac Ave., Lake Placid
full repair shop

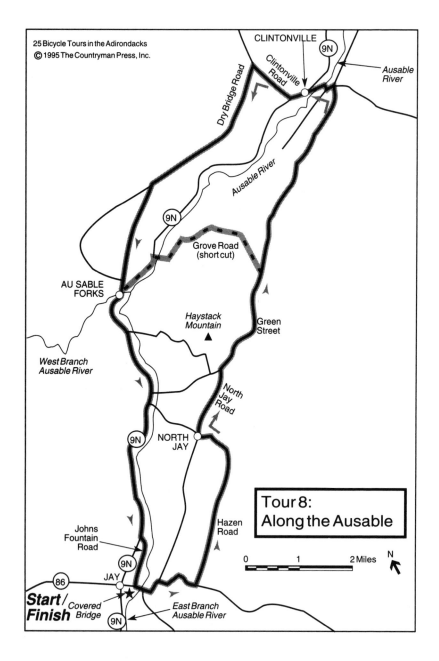

25 Bicycle Tours in the Adirondacks
© 1995 The Countryman Press, Inc.

CLINTONVILLE

9N

Ausable River

Dry Bridge Road

Clintonville Road

Ausable River

9N

Grove Road
(short cut)

AU SABLE
FORKS

Haystack
Mountain

Green
Street

West Branch
Ausable River

North
Jay
Road

9N

NORTH
JAY

Johns
Fountain
Road

Hazen
Road

Tour 8:
Along the Ausable

0   1   2 Miles

N

9N

86   JAY

Start /
Finish   Covered
Bridge

East Branch
Ausable River

9N

8
Along the Ausable

Distance: *25.3 miles*
Terrain: *Easy*

The Ausable River valley, much of which is covered in the course of this rambling ride, illustrates the fate of agriculture in the Adirondacks. A generation or two ago, this rich river-bottom valley, one of the best places in the Adirondacks for growing food, was crowded with small farmsteads. As a result of sanitation laws and ever-more-centralized agriculture, there is a single active dairy farmer left, a few people raising vegetables on a small scale, and one magnificent little farm growing perennial plants for the nursery trade. Jobs provided by prisons, hospitals, and colleges have filled the gap—many of the people in this valley work to the northeast in the city of Plattsburgh. And as a result, the pastures are increasingly growing in. This ride is utterly gorgeous now, but there may be fewer vistas in a few decades.

The ride starts in the town of Jay, an interesting little burg. A church has been converted to house the offices of *Adirondack Life,* the lovely magazine that celebrates the region every month. Next door, in an old dry-goods store, an eclectic combination of grungy antiques and spectacular pieces of handmade birchbark and twig furniture entice shoppers, and next door to that, at the Jay Craft Center, more modern arts and crafts are pursued. A general store, McDonalds, on the opposite corner is a good place to provision since you will not pass another business until the last third of the ride.

The real center of town, however, and the place where the ride begins, is a covered bridge just east of town—there are signs pointing the way, and revealing that it was built in 1857 and that it is the longest of its kind in New York State. What the signs won't tell you is that a few years ago state engineers decided it was necessary to build a new bridge just upstream, relegating the old one to, at best, a showpiece. Local people, joined by covered bridge aficionados from around the country, rose in opposition. Eventually, the state relented, and the old bridge has been reconditioned to make it stronger. With any luck, it will last for many more generations: New research in the Northeast is revealing that timber bridges are often more durable than the easily corroded steel replacements.

0.0   *Just across the bridge, a small park has places for several cars.*

Before starting out, and certainly after returning, you will want to take the time to explore the marvelous shelves and rapids just upstream of the bridge. Fly-fishermen are often at work there, and sometimes people are swimming, though caution is definitely advised in the swift current.

Leave the parking area following County Road 64 downstream (a left turn coming off the bridge), which in this part of the park means to the north.

0.4   *A state lot for anglers provides additional parking in case the park is crowded.*

0.5   *Turn right on Hazen Road, which will soon bear to the left and go uphill.*

In about 0.3 mile you'll pass the first field growing in to pine, a repeating sight along this tour. The pavement is bumpy and slow.

1.3   *Continue left on the main road.*

2.6   *Start downhill.*

In about 0.2 mile you will pass Aquidanick Farm on the left, a magical small farm specializing in perennial plants. Most of them are destined for nurseries downstate, but the owners also conduct a small retail trade and have a garden showing off their wares—as many as 250 different varieties.

3.2   *Marvelous views of hills suddenly become visible to the right.*

About a mile later, a new crag suddenly appears in the distance to the right—that's Haystack Mountain, which will dominate much of the next portion of the trip.

4.7   *Turn right onto North Jay Road, and begin a rolling ride through more farmland.*

The reconditioned covered bridge that marks the starting point of Tour 8 was built in 1857.

5.7 *A nicely maintained and shady graveyard offers a place to sit and rest.*

5.8 *Turn right on Green Street (there is no sign here), with Haystack looming up on the left.*

The road will wind up through a piney woods and then down to another set of semiopen fields, and here the cliffs are most visible and most impressive.

8.2 *Bear right at the intersection, following signs to Clintonville.*

(If you want to cut the ride shorter by a few miles, you can turn left instead, following the sign to Au Sable Forks. Be prepared for a fairly steep climb and a very steep descent to town; then follow the river until the first bridge, where you will cross and head straight through town to NY 9N, turning left for the ride back to Jay.)

9.1 *A gentle downhill begins and the pavement improves. The road* begins to wind, sometimes canting more steeply downhill, and occasionally offering views to the north.

11.6 The grade steepens considerably. Don't go too fast, for there is a stop sign waiting at the bottom.

11.8 Turn left at the stop sign, then take an immediate right across the bridge.

12.0 On the far side of the Ausable, turn left along the river.

12.3 Turn left onto NY 9N, which is a wider, busier road with a bad shoulder. Be extra careful—cars are fast and frequent.

12.6 Turn right on Clintonville Road, heading uphill. (You can continue along NY 9N and cut a bit off the trip, but Clintonville Road will be a less busy route.)

13.8 A sharp left turn following signs to Au Sable Forks on Dry Bridge Road. The road climbs slowly and steadily for about a mile, through scrubby and sandy terrain.

16.2 A smooth, gentle downhill begins, but beware—the shoulder is bad to nonexistent.

16.8 Bear left on the main road.

18.2 The grade steepens downhill, twisting, past a golf course.

18.8 A stop sign, and just across it you will find a playground offering a place to rest.

18.9 A Stewarts store offers an easy chance to reprovision. (For more substantial fare, a Grand Union is 0.2 mile ahead on the left.)

19.0 A bridge crosses the confluence of the East and West Branches of the Ausable.

You are heading into the downtown area of Au Sable Forks. A former mill town, Au Sable Forks gives the distinct impression of being somewhat down on its luck. Betsy Folwell, in her Adirondack guidebook, recommends the D&H Freight House Eatery on NY 9N for its "good diner chow, plus excellent inexpensive pizza," as well as for its railroad decor.

19.3 *Do not cross the bridge. Bear right instead on NY 9N.*

Remember all the earlier cautions about heavy traffic, bad shoulders, and so on. There is a phone booth about 0.1 mile ahead at the phone company office.

19.8 *A store offering an awesome selection of so-called "lawn cutouts." There are peeing children and bent-over plump adults of every gender and complexion, as well as bears, ducks, lawn jockeys, and assorted trolls.*

19.9 *Either the owner or the best customer of the above establishment has many of the lawn decorations out front—note especially the California Raisin, whose legs rotate feverishly in the wind.*

20.3 *A long stretch of river comes into view—you will track pretty close to the Ausable all the rest of the way back to Jay.*

21.3 *A bridge offers a place to sit and eat or to just stare at the meandering river.*

22.2 *A turnout, designed to allow the Jay Volunteer Fire Company access to the river so they can fill their tanker, offers another natural spot to stop. The views improve constantly to the south and east, and indeed a local developer is offering acreage with a big sign that sports the slogan "Buy a View, Lots for You."*

24.2 *Left on Johns Fountain Road, heading downhill.*

Caution: Be extremely careful crossing the road.

25.2 *Left across the covered bridge.*

This is a one-lane bridge. Be cautious, and if a car is approaching from the other side let it go through first. You will want to be unhurried as you ride or walk your bike through, savoring the light filtering in through the gaps in the boards. The parking lot is just to the left as you come out the other side of the bridge. There are picnic tables there, but really—take your lunch down to the rocks on the river.

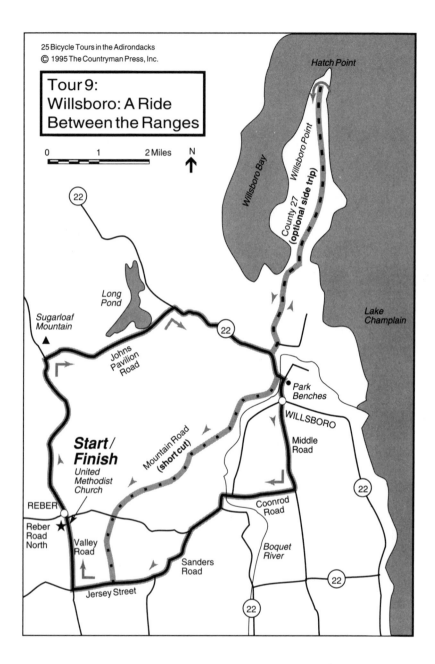

25 Bicycle Tours in the Adirondacks
© 1995 The Countryman Press, Inc.

Tour 9:
Willsboro: A Ride
Between the Ranges

0   1   2 Miles

N

22

Hatch Point

Willsboro Bay

Willsboro Point

County 27 **(optional side trip)**

Lake Champlain

Long Pond

Sugarloaf Mountain

Johns Pavilion Road

22

Park Benches

WILLSBORO

Middle Road

Start / Finish
United Methodist Church

Mountain Road **(short cut)**

REBER

Reber Road North

Valley Road

Coonrod Road

Boquet River

22

Sanders Road

Jersey Street

22

22

9

Willsboro: A Ride Between the Ranges

Distance: *18.3 miles*
Terrain: *Relatively easy, with only a few hills*

Those who live in New York City are perhaps aware of the Long Island City phenomenon. Because Manhattan's enormous buildings make seeing more than a block difficult, it is widely conceded that the best view of the great city is from Long Island City, just across the East River in unglamorous Queens. Something the same could be said of the Adirondacks. Stuck down among the trees, a cyclist often has difficulty seeing even the nearby mountains, and vistas are hard to come by unless you're willing to hike to an open peak. Viewed from the east side of Lake Champlain, however, the mountains rise up in all their granite glory. Vermont: the Queens of the Adirondacks.

For those unwilling to make the trip to the Green Mountain State, though, this ride in Willsboro offers nearly as magnificent a view—and as an added bonus it also affords several sweeping panoramas of Camel's Hump, Mt. Mansfield, and the other high peaks of Vermont. In fact, at one spot along the ride you can see the two ranges at once, just by turning your head.

The route is Vermontlike in other ways as well. The valley is narrower on the New York side of Lake Champlain, but it is also heavily agricultural, and much of this route runs alongside open fields, where depending on the season you may see hay being cut to feed the dairy cows that are the principal means of support. (You will also see many fields growing in to trees and brush—the ruinous economics of the dairy industry, exacerbated in recent years with the advent of bovine growth hormone and other misguided feats of genetic engineering, mean that fewer and fewer small farmers can stay in business. As a direct result, it is quite likely that the vistas along this ride will be much reduced in a generation, and possible that much of the area will return to forest in years to come.)

Lake Champlain moderates temperatures year-round—this ride will stay comfortable into the late fall, when you may find snow falling in other parts of the Adirondacks, and the drifts will melt here much earlier than other places, making this an excellent early-season tuneup. Most of the roads on this tour, except those leading in and out of the town of Willsboro, should be fairly free of cars throughout the year; after Labor Day you'll often have the road to yourself.

0.0 *A very good place to start this tour is the Reber United Methodist Church, mainly because it means you will end your loop with a long and spectacular downhill plunge.*

(The church parking lot is usually deserted, but on Sunday morning you might want to consider starting elsewhere—perhaps in the town of Willsboro, where there is also ample parking.) To reach the Reber church, follow signs from Northway exit 32 east toward Willsboro. Turn left onto Valley Road, and follow it downhill to the church, about a mile. The church has a distinctive yellow tin steeple.

Once aboard your bicycle, turn right out of the church parking lot, crossing a small creek almost immediately.

0.4 *The road forks. Do not take the right-hand turn to Willsboro unless you want to cut several miles off the trip. Instead, bear left on Reber Road North.*

0.6 *Pass a wonderful dairy barn on the left (breathe deep; this is a working farm) and an even more picturesque defunct ivy-covered barn on the right.*

Several more farms dot the road for the next mile or so, including the quite lovely Cold Brook Farm at 1.4 miles.

1.7 *Begin a descent, around a right-hand curve and passing a burned-out farmhouse on the right; trees are beginning to grow up from inside the old house.*

2.2 *The road heads out of the open and into the woods. It winds up and down (more up than down). While it is paved, the pave-*

ment is worn and patched in many spots, so keep your eyes on the road, not on the young softwood forest on either side.

3.7 *As you begin to head downhill, you will see the cliffs on Sugarloaf Mountain directly ahead of you.*

5.8 *Pass a small farm with horses.*

6.2 *You will see Long Pond on your left.*

One of the potential access points to Long Pond is marked "No Parking, No Trespassing," while the other one is not marked anything at all. Betsy Folwell, in her invaluable guide *The Adirondack Book*, recommends spending the night at Long Pond Cabins, which are on NY 22, a bit ahead. The cabins, open from April through October, offer boat rentals (518-963-7269).

6.7 *Turn right at the stop sign onto NY 22. Traffic may be considerably heavier here; there is a shoulder, albeit a narrow one.*

7.3 *Begin a mile-long downhill.*

7.7 *Lake Champlain, and behind it the distinctive shape of Camel's Hump, sweep into dramatic view.*

8.3 *The downhill ends, and you pass under a railroad bridge.*

9.0 *Continue straight on NY 22.*

The road on your left heads toward Willsboro Bay, a particularly lovely stretch of the Champlain shoreline, which on several occasions in American history would have afforded views of grand naval engagements (the American navy had its birth not far south of here, at Whitehall). On a pretty day, you might want to consider extending your trip with a jaunt on County Road 27 to the end of Willsboro Point and back. On the right at this junction is Ethel's Dew Drop Inn, which has a takeout window.

9.4 *Start steeply downhill, and around a sharp left-hand turn into town.*

9.6 *Pass Mountain Road on the right. If you want to cut short the loop, this will return you fairly quickly to the Reber intersection and church.*

9.7 *Cross the Boquet River (pronounced bo-KET).*

Here, at the center of Willsboro, you will find several war memorials on a small plaza above the river, and a couple of lovely swinging benches on which to sit. Across the street, a small plaque commemorates the encampment of British general John Burgoyne at this spot in the summer of 1777, as he attempted to open a route between Canada and New York. The plaque gives scant detail. It was here that Burgoyne, at the head of some 7000 troops, summoned 400 Indians to a "war feast," at which he made the somewhat contradictory pleas that they rout the rebels but at the same time do so humanely. "It is nobler to spare than to revenge, to discriminate degrees of guilt, to suspend the uplifted stroke, to chastise and not destroy," he announced in his curious sermonette.

9.8 *A Grand Union supermarket offers the best chance for provisioning, and across the street a hardware store offers some supplies that might be useful in repairs.*

10.0 *At Brown House Antiques, begin to climb the hill out of town.*

10.1 *Turn right onto Middle Road.*

11.0 *If you strain your neck to the right, the first views of the Adirondacks will appear, a taste of what's to come.*

11.2 *A short steep climb brings you to the height-of-land, and excellent views to both sides.*

In the late afternoon, you'll often see the Adirondacks framed in the "god rays" of the dropping sun; to the right, all the ridges leading up out of Lake Champlain to the highest point in Vermont, Mt. Mansfield, are clearly visible.

11.9 *Another gorgeous view to the left, this time complemented by a picturesque farm and a delicious-looking array of produce at a small farm stand.*

12.0 *Turn right onto Coonrod Road, heading due west and right at the High Peaks of the Adirondacks, especially that section around magnificent Giant Mountain. For the next mile, as you run between hayfields, you will be hard-pressed to take your eyes off the mountains; this is a view of Coloradan proportions.*

12.4 *Look down long enough to negotiate a bumpy railroad crossing.*

13.0 *Descend somewhat, into the woods, and past abandoned*

Authors Mitchell Hay and Barbara Lemmel on their tandem bike

67

fields now grown into goldenrod. The route crosses a bridge on the Boquet at 13.3.

14.3 *Turn left on Sanders Road, and climb steeply for 0.3 mile. After the climb, the road winds gently through young woods.*

15.8 *Bear right on Jersey Street, which is also known as County Road 12. (The road is not marked at this junction.)*

16.2 *The horse-crossing sign here shows a draft horse, not a thoroughbred. In fact, you will see both in the fields that line either side of the road, and you will also see more views of the High Peaks as you ride gently downhill.*

17.3 *Turn right onto Valley Road, passing a riding stable on your right and a hayfield on your left.*

You will begin a long descent: stop pedaling, and gaze out at about 11 o'clock to the cliff-studded face of Poke-O-Moonshine Mountain. The name is probably a corruption of the Native American words for rocky and smooth, an apt description for this distinctive chunk of rock, much loved by rock climbers for its many routes. Hikers like it also, for it rewards their efforts with a view from a fire tower of this whole lovely Champlain Valley region.

18.3 *Return to the Reber Church.*

10

Westport–Essex: Farmland and Lakefront

Distance: *23.7 miles*
Terrain: *Moderately rolling, with a couple of steep climbs*

The sport cyclists of Westport have the prettiest 24-mile workout loop of anyone we know. This ride is a perfect mix of flat and rolly terrain, with two memorable climbs toward the end. Nestled in the Champlain Valley, where agriculture is not so difficult as in the more mountainous regions of the Adirondack Park, open fields afford many spectacular views of the Adirondack Mountains to the west, and of the Green Mountains of Vermont to the east. On this route, you will enjoy views of Vermont as you ride north. Once you turn south, the High Peaks will greet you.

The town of Westport was settled in 1770 and was a thriving port in the last century, shipping out the lumber, iron, wool, and agricultural products produced inland in the Adirondacks. A ferry service took passengers across Lake Champlain, to and from Vermont, as early as 1820. Many of the old homes reflect the Gothic style of that era.

Westport became a summer vacation spot just after the Civil War, and its popularity continues. As a result, it boasts shops and restaurants unusual in the Adirondacks. It is possible, for instance, to buy fine wines at Westport Bay Wine and Spirits, just down the road from Ron's Fishing Hole, the local live bait shop. Be sure to stop in at the Westport Trading Co. on Main Street, where Kip Trienens creates spectacular stained-glass windows, panels, and mirrors.

If you are staying at one of the town's inns or bed & breakfast establishments, be sure to ask for a schedule of performances at the Meadowmount School of Music, located just out of town. Its alumni include Yo-Yo Ma, Itzhak Perlman, Pinchas Zukerman, and others; both faculty and

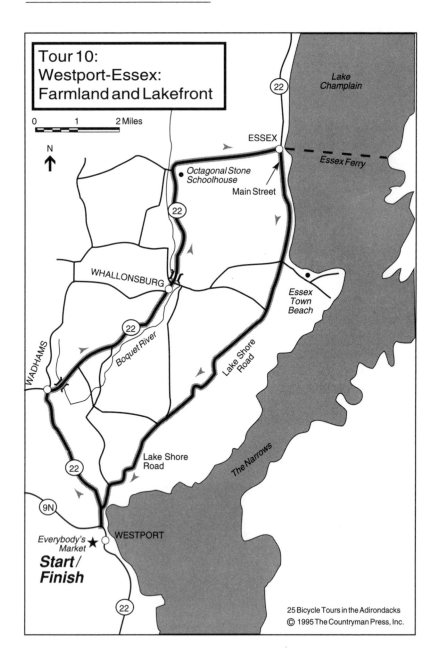

Tour 10:
Westport-Essex:
Farmland and Lakefront

0 1 2 Miles

N

Lake Champlain

ESSEX

Essex Ferry

Octagonal Stone Schoolhouse

Main Street

WHALLONSBURG

Essex Town Beach

WADHAMS

Boquet River

Lake Shore Road

The Narrows

Lake Shore Road

9N

Everybody's Market

WESTPORT

Start / Finish

25 Bicycle Tours in the Adirondacks
© 1995 The Countryman Press, Inc.

students give free concerts. Or, for more homegrown entertainment, try the Depot Theatre, which produces several plays and musicals each summer, including at least one produced and performed exclusively by young people from the area, through the theatre's Summer Apprentice Program.

This 24-mile tour begins and ends at Everybody's Market, a friendly grocery store in the middle of town. The folks who work here are happy to fill water bottles, give directions, or help with anything else you may need. You may park in their lot, but be sure to ask permission first.

0.0   Begin traveling north on NY 22.

In a few hundred feet you can see across Lake Champlain from the boat launch.

0.4   Pass by Lake Shore Road on your right.

This is the road by which you'll return in a couple of dozen miles.

0.5   You are not yet warmed up, but you have to climb a fairly serious 0.6-mile hill to get out of town. You will be warmed up once you reach the top, however.

1.8   Cross over railroad tracks.

The scenery here is typical of the Champlain Valley. The eye is treated to a patchwork of hay- and cornfields, a visual cacophony of wildflowers, cows contentedly munching away, secretly jealous that their Vermont sisters get better press, and graying barns slowly losing their grip on the vertical.

3.3   Enjoy a sweeping curve of downhill into the hamlet of Wadhams.

The lovely Boquet River bends along the road on your right.

3.6   Cross over the bridge spanning the Boquet River.

Stop for a moment to enjoy the falls. Be sure to take a quick loop around the Wadhams village green and take in the architecture and ambience of this hamlet.

As you leave Wadhams, the terrain becomes decidedly roller-coasterlike.

5.7   Cross the Essex town line. The Boquet River continues to flow on your right.

7.4   Enter the hamlet of Whallonsburg. Stay on NY 22.

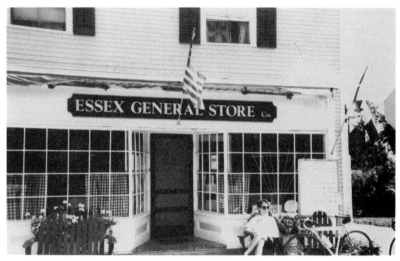

Relaxing at the Essex General Store

7.7 *Cross over the bridge and begin a steady, gentle climb.*

8.2 *Pass by the Boquet River Ranch on your left.*

Their sign proclaims "Spanish Mustangs."

9.6 *As you look across the field to your right you can get a magnificent view of Vermont's Camel's Hump mountain and Mt. Mansfield, that state's highest peak.*

10.5 *NY 22 takes a hard right turn.*

Right after the turn, notice the unusual octagonal stone school building on the right. Built in 1826, the Boquet Octagonal Schoolhouse was in use for classes until the 1950s. By 1995 it should be restored and open to the public.

11.4 *Hoof it up to the top of this short, steep rise. Descend into downtown Essex.*

Here is a wonderful view of Lake Champlain and the valley below you. The Green Mountains of Vermont stretch north to south from horizon to horizon.

13.0 *At the T intersection, turn right onto Main Street.*

The town of Essex is an Adirondack architecture buff's dream.

Burned to the ground by General Burgoyne 2 centuries ago, Essex was a prosperous shipbuilding, quarrying, and mining town by the mid-1800s. The rise of rail and the downfall of canal-based commerce meant that Essex lost population for the next century. The happy side effect of past economic downfall is that Essex boasts an amazing collection of pre–Civil War architecture.

The Essex Community Heritage Organization (518-963-7088) provides a pamphlet for self-guided tours of the homes and inns and schools from the 18th and 19th centuries. Change your cleats for a pair of sandals and enjoy a walk through the past.

Minor food cravings can be satisfied at the general store, or by taking a left at the T intersection and having lunch at the Old Dock Restaurant. Here you can watch the ferries shuttle folk across Lake Champlain to Charlotte, Vermont. Head south on Main Street.

You will encounter an uphill out of town, but then you can enjoy the homes, sailboats, and views of the lake along the relatively flat plateau.

15.6 *You'll encounter a three-way intersection as the road reaches lake level. Go straight to continue the tour.*

While there is no sign announcing the change, Main Street has become Lake Shore Road. If you want to take a swim, turn left for the public beach.

15.8 *Begin a long, steep climb up from the lake back into the Adirondack foothills.*

16.5 *Top of the hill.*

Through your hypoxic haze you can admire the view of the Adirondack Mountains to your right.

19.2 *Begin another uphill climb. This one is about 0.3 mile long.*

20.7 *Begin a well-deserved 3-mile downhill into Westport.*

23.3 *At the intersection with NY 22 turn left into Westport.*

23.7 *Return to Everybody's Market.*

There is a pasta and pizza place next door, or you can continue south on NY 22 for more shops, restaurants, and the village Green.

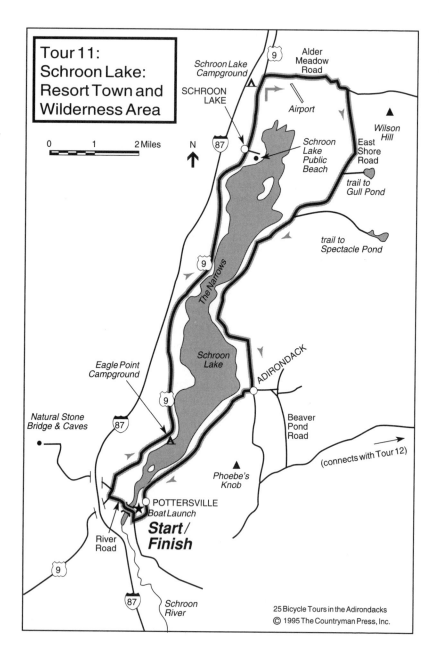

Tour 11:
Schroon Lake:
Resort Town and
Wilderness Area

0   1   2 Miles

N

Alder
Meadow
Road

9

Schroon Lake
Campground

SCHROON
LAKE

87

Airport

Schroon
Lake
Public
Beach

Wilson
Hill

East
Shore
Road

trail to
Gull Pond

trail to
Spectacle Pond

9

The Narrows

Schroon
Lake

Eagle Point
Campground

ADIRONDACK

9

Natural Stone
Bridge & Caves

87

Beaver
Pond
Road

(connects with Tour 12)

Phoebe's
Knob

POTTERSVILLE
Boat Launch

Start /
Finish

River
Road

9

87

Schroon
River

25 Bicycle Tours in the Adirondacks
© 1995 The Countryman Press, Inc.

11
Schroon Lake:
Resort Town and Wilderness Area

Distance: *26.1 miles*
Terrain: *Moderately hilly, with a couple of steep climbs*

Like many of the bodies of water in the Adirondack Park, Schroon Lake is long and narrow, reaching 9 miles from the south-southwestern tip to the north-northeastern end. At its widest, it is only 1.5 miles across, and at the narrowest point (called, appropriately enough, "the Narrows"), less than 0.25 separates the east and west shores.

Schroon Lake is also strikingly beautiful. Viewed from the more-inhabited west side, a series of mountains stretch along the eastern shore, from Phoebe's Knob to Wilson Hill. Sunrise and moonrise are both spectacular, particularly when the lake is still and reflecting the beauty of both hill and sky. During the day, the lake is busy with motorboats and jet skis and sailboats; in the quieter mornings and evenings, canoeists ply the water in search of views, exercise, and fish.

During the early part of the last century, some of the first timber cut and shipped out of the Adirondacks was felled near Schroon Lake, run down the Schroon River to the Hudson, and then delivered south to build scaffolding in New York City. The timber and tanning industries played an important role in the development of the hamlet of Schroon Lake and the surrounding towns. The lake's beauty, as well as its usefulness, served the area well; tourists boarded steamboats in Pottersville at the southern tip of the lake and were ferried in grand style to resorts and boardinghouses in the towns of Schroon Lake and Adirondack.

Today, the hamlet of Schroon Lake is the largest town in the area, and tourism remains an important part of the town's livelihood. There are many hotels, bed & breakfasts, and campgrounds in and near the town, and restaurants range from basic diners to fancy European-style establishments. Of the former, Pitkin's Restaurant is probably the best, with inexpensive, hearty fare and a Texas-style barbecue that's hard to beat in this part of the country. On the other end of the scale, the Schroon Lake Inn (518-532-7042), a couple miles north of town, features elegant cuisine served on the veranda, overlooking Schroon Lake in all its glory.

In addition, you'll find a Grand Union grocery store, several outdoor outfitters that can supply you with maps, camping supplies, and fishing tackle, a laundromat, and just about anything else you might need— except a bike shop.

If you're staying in the area, you might want to take advantage of the cultural opportunities in the town. The Schroon Lake Arts Council hosts concerts and dance performances, and a folk music weekend festival in August. In addition, the Seagle Colony, founded by tenor Oscar Seagle, features vespers services on Sunday evenings.

The bike loop begins at the Schroon Lake boat launch at the southern tip of the lake, just half a mile east of US 9 on River Road. The launch has ample parking and public washrooms, making it a good place to begin and end your ride.

0.0   **Turn right out of the boat launch parking lot onto River Road.**

As you cross the bridge, notice the Schroon River flowing to your left; often you will see folks fishing, sunning, and picnicking on the river's banks.

Just 0.2 mile farther, you will see the first of many signs for Word of Life, an evangelical Christian group that has its international headquarters on the southwestern shore of Schroon Lake.

0.6   **Turn right onto US 9.**

The next 10 miles or so are the least enjoyable part of the ride, and it is good to get them out of the way early. US 9 carries a fair amount of traffic, and the shoulders are not in good condition. The terrain is rolling, with several long but gentle climbs.

0.8   **Note the sign for the Natural Stone Bridge and Caves, to the left.**

This tourist attraction features a variety of interesting rock formations, including five caves. The gift shop offers minerals, crystals, and fossils, with demonstrations of rock-cutting techniques.

2.5   **Eagle Point Campground and Day-Use Area is on the right.**

The state-run campground is squeezed tightly between US 9 and Schroon Lake. The campground facilities are good, but no site is free from the noise of semitrailers rumbling by on one side, and speedboats whizzing by on the other. Eagle Point also features what must be the smallest swimming area in all the Adirondacks; it's hard to do much more than wade in the designated area, and the lifeguards won't allow swimming outside the ropes. Wait to take a dip at the public beach in the hamlet of Schroon Lake.

6.4   The Narrows Restaurant, on the right, serves pizza and ice cream, and has a great view of the lake from its parking lot.

9.1   Enter the hamlet of Schroon Lake.

The public beach is just 0.1 mile into town, on the right. Traffic through town can be congested, with street parking on both sides of the road and many pedestrians going to and from the town's shops and restaurants.

9.8   As you leave town, you will begin a 1-mile climb that is the most challenging so far in the ride.

10.5   The Schroon Lake Campground, on your left, is not on the shore of the lake, but is much quieter than Eagle Point.

11.1   At the bottom of the hill, turn right onto Alder Meadow Road, following the sign to the municipal airport.

11.7   Note the grassy airfield on the right, with its wind socks informing you whether you have a headwind or tailwind.

12.8   The scenery opens a bit as you pass through a marsh, offering views of the Schroon Valley to the north and south. The road climbs after the marsh.

13.2   Still climbing, turn right onto East Shore Road.

As you ride along this road, the number of homes will diminish rapidly. For most of the next 7 miles, the woods to the right of the road are state forest preserve, and to the left the land is designated wilderness area. The road is sparsely traveled and is quite narrow. Even at midday, the pavement is quite well shaded by the trees, and the effect is of riding through the forest itself. If you pay close attention, you will see jack-in-the-pulpits along the road, a rare find in this area.

Riding along the Schroon River

Culverts frequently cross the road, and in places the pavement has settled around them, creating "speed bumps" that can be jarring if you're not watching for them.

14.2 *At last, you reach the top of the hill you began climbing just past the airfield.*

You can see Wilson Hill to the left, the most northern mountain along Schroon Lake.

14.9 *Note the trailhead on the left to Gull Pond, just 0.5 mile from the road.*

15.9 *This trailhead leads to Spectacle Pond, so named because its shape vaguely resembles a pair of eyeglasses.*

16.7 *Leaving the forest preserve, you will note homes on the right, along the lake. The road becomes increasingly hilly, with steeper climbs and descents.*

19.0 *A steep uphill ends just 0.3 mile later.*

20.5 *This last hill of the route is also steep, and 0.5 mile long. It ends in the hamlet of Adirondack.*

This hamlet was originally called Mill Brook, but when the federal postal service began to establish zip codes, it was discovered that another New York town named Mill Brook had already been given a zip code. The residents had to come up with a new name quickly, and Adirondack seemed to fit quite nicely.

This town had its heyday in the tanning and logging days. It was also a favorite stop of steamboating tourists. Now the small hamlet is home to many summer residents, as well as a hardy year-round population.

21.7 *Stop at the Adirondack General Store, on your left, for food, bathrooms, and conversation.*

A visit to the Adirondack General Store makes all the hills you've just climbed worthwhile. Owners Joan and Dick Lomnitzer operate a combination deli/restaurant/grocery store/craft shop that manages to cover all your needs at once. The food is good, inexpensive, and served with a smile; if they're not busy, Joan and Dick will sit and chat with you for a while. They can be busy, though; a typical summer Sunday finds them serving 70 or 80 breakfasts at the store's four tables.

The store has been in this building, under a variety of owners, for 150 years. With just a little prodding, Dick will show you pictures from the store's and town's history. He can also explain the game "skittles," which was popularized here, and was a kind of vertical bowling using 4-foot bowling pins and a heavy wooden bowling ball suspended on a chain. It's since been shrunk to a board game, but must have been impressive in its original scale.

21.8 *Turn right at the intersection just past the general store, heading downhill to Schroon Lake. At the water, bear left.*

The next 4 miles are nearly flat, and travel right along the shore of the lake. Lovely homes line the road, with boats bobbing peacefully at private docks.

26.0 *Turn right onto River Road, at the southern end of Schroon Lake.*

26.1 *Return to the parking lot of the Schroon Lake boat launch.*

79

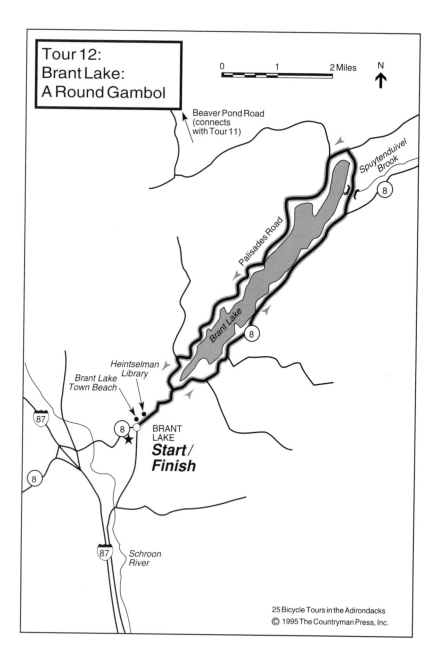

Tour 12:
Brant Lake:
A Round Gambol

0   1   2 Miles

N

Beaver Pond Road
(connects
with Tour 11)

Spuytenduivel Brook

8

Palisades Road

Brant Lake

8

Heintselman Library

Brant Lake Town Beach

87

8

8

BRANT LAKE

*Start /
Finish*

Schroon River

87

25 Bicycle Tours in the Adirondacks
© 1995 The Countryman Press, Inc.

80

12
Brant Lake: A Round Gambol

Distance: 15 miles
Terrain: An easy road trip with almost no ups or downs

Brant Lake is a town that requires travelers to slow down and take a look, if only because NY 8, which passes through the town, takes a 90-degree turn that requires even the most seasoned driver to take it easy through town. Fortunately, it's a town that is worth slowing down to see. The businesses and churches are clustered around the stillness of Mill Pond, giving the downtown an open, charming feeling.

Like many towns in this part of the Adirondacks, Brant Lake was a logging encampment in the 1800s. Trees were cut around the lake, floated down to Mill Pond, and held until springtime. When the spring waters were at their peak, the dam to Mill Pond was opened, and the logs rushed downstream to the Schroon River, where they journeyed south to Glens Falls and beyond. Any logs that didn't make it out when the dam was opened were saved in the pond until the next year. Occasionally, a log would sink, and when the town drained the pond a couple of years ago to repair the pond's fountain, there were quite a few hundred-year-old logs sitting on the bottom.

In the late 1800s, a tannery was built in Brant Lake that eventually grew to be the largest in New York State. As the supply of native hemlocks declined (hemlock bark was the source of tannin used in processing the hides), however, so did the tanning industry. The town is now considerably smaller than it once was.

0.0 Begin riding south on Market Street from the Town Hall, with Mill Pond on your left.

0.1 At the dam and waterfall on the end of Mill Pond, turn left onto NY 8.

The dam at the end of Mill Pond in Brant Lake

0.2 *Daby's General Store, on the right, is an old-fashioned establishment that supplies just about anything you might need, from groceries to camping supplies to clothing. The town beach is on your left.*

0.4 *Note the sign above the garage at Doug's Auto Repair, which reads "Lubritory." Anyone in search of refurbished Corvairs will do well to take a look here. The Horicon Baptist Church sign declares "Strangers Welcome."*

But by far the greatest treasure of this downtown area is the Heintselman Library, on the left, across from the Baptist church. It was built in 1907 on the insistence of Mrs. Heintselman, who decided the town needed a library, donated books of her own, and held library fund-raising dances that charged a book for the library as admission. The library building was built right out onto the pond, and the entire building is of local stone; even the sign on the library is created out of stones.

A delightful winding road brings you out of the village. To the left, on the water that drains into Mill Pond, nearly every home has its own boating dock extending into the lily pads and the smooth, clear water.

0.7 *Note the Horicon Museum on your right, which houses historical artifacts and pictures of the town.*

1.2 *At this end of Brant Lake (the lake, not the town), NY 8 bends to the right; follow it so that the lake remains on your left.*

The road along the lake is winding and can carry quite a bit of truck traffic. The shoulder is narrow. The lovely views of the lake, with its many estates and more modest homes, many of which are bordered by white picket fences, make this route worth the traffic.

2.6 *Note the Point o' Pines Camp for Girls on the left.*

There are a number of group camps and retreat centers on this lake. Brant Lake Camp, on your right a couple of miles farther down the road, is a marvelous old estate, still in use.

6.3 *Turn left on Palisades Road. The traffic all but vanishes once you leave NY 8.*

6.6 *Cross the bridge over the Spuytenduivel Brook, which flows* *into Brant Lake. The bridge offers terrific views of the surrounding mountains in both directions.*

Perhaps the brook is named after Spuyten Duyvil Creek, which flows into the Hudson, hundreds of miles from here. In his tales, Washington Irving translates the name as "in spite of the devil."

7.8 *If you wish to combine this route with the Schroon Lake Loop, turn right at Beaver Pond Road. To continue around Brant Lake, stay on Palisades Road.*

9.1 *A marsh opens on both sides of the road, providing views of the mountains to the north and the lake to the south.*

10.7 *Palisades Road becomes more narrow here, really not much more than a glorified driveway.*

12.7 *If you look across the lake, you will see a house built on an island in the lake. Canada geese often stop here on their migrations.*

14.0 *Cross the bridge over the flow that runs from Brant Lake to Mill Pond.*

14.2 *Turn right onto NY 8 to return to the town of Brant Lake.*

14.9 *Turn right onto Market Street, at the head of Mill Pond.*

15.0 *Return to the town hall.*

LAKE GEORGE AND ENVIRONS

Lake George and Environs: Lake Luzerne, Bolton Landing, and Pilot Knob Loop

Three tours begin in the historic village of Lake George, located on the southwest corner of Lake George itself. The lake stretches for some 27 miles north-northwest along the eastern region of the Adirondack Park, and is nearly 2 miles across at its widest point. Mountains border the lake on both sides, offering spectacular views from almost any point along the water.

The lake has always been a significant travel corridor for the inhabitants of the region, and the area figured prominently in the French and Indian Wars in the 1750s. Twice British armies rowed from the southern end of the lake, in a flotilla that reached from shore to shore for as far as the eye could see, to attack the French fort at Ticonderoga at the far northern end of the lake. Fort William Henry, located in what is now the village of Lake George, was the base of these attacks. In 1755, General Montcalm attacked the fort with French and Indian forces. Montcalm, according to history, had planned an organized defeat, but the Indian troops massacred the surrendering British troops and burned the fort to the ground. Today, the fort has been restored and is open for tours, and banners hang in front declaring, "Home of The Last of the Mohicans."

The Fort William Henry Motor Inn, located next door to the restored fort, is evidence of the town's next identity, that of resort community. By 1800, the first resort had been built on the lake, farther north at Bolton Landing, and by 1817, the first steamboat was plying the river from Lake George Village northward, bringing city travelers to this idyllic country setting. Tourism has defined the landscape ever since. In a village that got its start during the French and Indian Wars, it is the T-shirt shop wars that now rage along its main thoroughfare. The downtown specializes in kitsch, its shops brimming with trinkets and souvenirs, its storefronts home to psychics and other purveyors of the paranormal, and its museums the kind that boast wax models of Frankenstein. To the north and south of the downtown area, strips of hotels, motels, and cabins line the road and the lakeshore.

If all of this sounds like the kind of tourist trap you came to the Adirondacks to avoid, don't despair. With so many shops concentrated in Lake George, the rest of the region is remarkably free of such clutter. Indeed, on all three of these bike tours you will begin in the traffic and bustle of Lake George Village, and move quickly into the "real" Adirondacks of peaceful roads and small towns, before returning to your starting point. The village also contains a bike shop, FlipFlop Cycleshop, located in a small mall across from the post office.

When planning your ride, be aware that traffic in Lake George Village varies with the season. Between Memorial Day and Labor Day, the village itself and the surrounding roads will be full of cars, particularly on weekends. During the fall and spring, however, most of the shops and motels are closed, and the traffic is much lighter; on some weekdays you will have the town virtually to yourself. The exception to this rule is the fall foliage season, when drivers again flock to the region to admire the changing colors along the lake's mountains.

All three tours begin at the Old Warren County Courthouse, home to the Lake George Historical Association Museum and Bookstore, at the corner of Canada and Amherst Streets. Metered parking is available on the main streets, in the town parking lots, and on some side streets; with some hunting, you should be able to find free street parking not far from the courthouse.

Bike Shops

FlipFlop Cycleshop
175 Canada St., Maynard Center, Lake George
518-668-2233

Rick's Bike Shop
Intersection of Ridge and Quaker, Glens Falls
518-793-8986

13
Lake Luzerne:
New York State's Dude Ranch Trail

Distance: *38.2 miles*
Terrain: *Moderate*

This route follows an already designated auto route, the New York State Dude Ranch Trail. Though few of the original dude ranches are in evidence today, there is still an occasional working ranch and rodeo along the way.

0.0 *Begin at the Old Warren County Courthouse, corner of Canada and Amherst Streets. Ride south (keeping the lake on your left) out of town on US 9 (Canada Street).*

0.6 *Note the left turn to the Lake George public beach (Million Dollar Beach).*

On a hot summer afternoon, you may wish to return here after your ride for a swim and well-deserved loll on the beach.

0.8 *The state-run Lake George Battleground Campground is on the left.*

This camp offers the closest camping to the village; however, in the summer it is often full, and the sound of auto traffic is never far away.

1.5 *Turn right onto NY 9N South, toward Lake Luzerne.*

This is also the turn for the Northway, I-87. After the Northway ramps the traffic will decrease considerably for the rest of the ride.

As you turn onto NY 9N, you will begin a steady climb toward Lake Luzerne. The first hill is the steepest, though not terribly difficult. As you move farther from Lake George, you will find your-

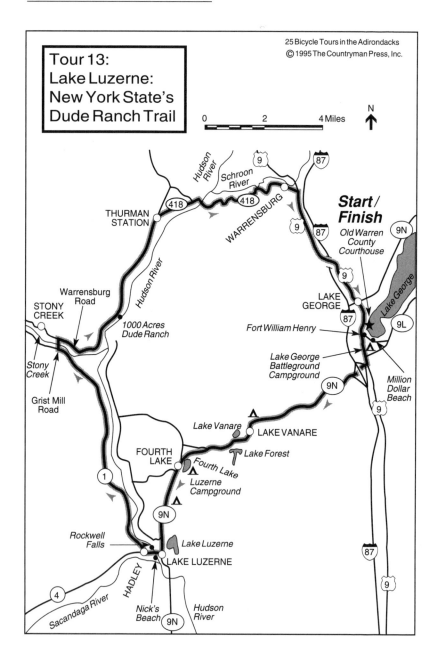

Tour 13:
Lake Luzerne:
New York State's
Dude Ranch Trail

25 Bicycle Tours in the Adirondacks
© 1995 The Countryman Press, Inc.

0   2   4 Miles

N

Hudson River
Schroon River

418   418   WARRENSBURG

9   87

**Start /
Finish**

9N

THURMAN
STATION

Old Warren
County
Courthouse

9

Warrensburg
Road

Hudson River

LAKE
GEORGE

87

9L

Lake George

STONY
CREEK

1000 Acres
Dude Ranch

Fort William Henry

Stony
Creek

Lake George
Battleground
Campground

Million
Dollar
Beach

Grist Mill
Road

9N

9

Lake Vanare   LAKE VANARE

FOURTH
LAKE

Lake Forest

1

Fourth Lake

Luzerne
Campground

9N

Rockwell
Falls

Lake Luzerne

87

HADLEY

LAKE LUZERNE

9

4

Sacandaga River

Nick's
Beach

9N

Hudson
River

self surrounded by woods on either side of the road, broken only by occasional driveways and signs advertising scenic homes and summer getaways. There is an acceptable 1-meter shoulder for the next few miles.

3.1 *This is the top of the first rise out of Lake George.*

The remaining hills are shorter and less steep, though the terrain does continue to rise gently for the next several miles.

5.1 *Pass the "Entering Lake Luzerne" sign.*

The road conditions improve considerably, with a wider shoulder and better pavement. Several campgrounds are located along this road.

6.2 *Enter the village of Lake Vanare, containing cottages, hotels, and a riding stable.*

6.5 *To the right, you can glimpse the peaceful Lake Vanare.*

A diner and general store are located on the left. The bridge crosses a small channel that connects Lake Vanare with Lake Forest, another small lake not visible from NY 9N. Cottages and homes dot the shores of both lakes.

7.5 *Pass a roadside rest area on the right.*

There are picnic tables and a place to pull off the road, but not much in the way of scenic views. A visitors information center is across the road.

8.8 *Enter Fourth Lake, another small, peaceful resort town on the shore of its namesake.*

Just 0.1 mile later, the Lake Luzerne Public Campground and Day-Use Area access road turns off to the left. The Harris Grocery Store stocks the basics and is a good place to stop for a quick snack if you feel the need, but buy something you can carry and bring it along to Lake Luzerne, where there is a good picnic spot. Once you leave Fourth Lake, the view opens to the right to the surrounding mountains.

11.8 *At the Hadley-Luzerne Central School, turn right onto Mill Street; a sign directs you to the Lake Luzerne Business District.*

After the turn, Nick's Beach will be on your left. This shady park lies along the stream that flows from Lake Luzerne into the Hudson River and is an excellent place to stop for a rest and a snack.

12.0 Turn left onto Main Street.

This is the business district of the village of Lake Luzerne, containing small shops, Papa's Ice Cream Parlor, and the historical society museum.

Lake Luzerne earned its living in the early days from the Hudson River, which was a watery thoroughfare for the timber industry. Wood pulp, used in making paper, was produced in Lake Luzerne, bringing considerable wealth into the town. The village boasts many fine old homes, several in the Victorian style, and beautiful stone churches. It, too, is now a resort community, though much quieter than Lake George.

12.3 Turn right at Stone's Pharmacy.

Note the graceful stone architecture of the Rockwell Falls Presbyterian Church on your left after the turn.

12.4 Cross over the Hudson River bridge.

Stop on the bridge over the Hudson River and note, upstream, the Rockwell Falls, which flow between dramatic outcroppings of granite. Turn to look downstream, and you will glimpse the confluence of the Hudson and the Sacandaga Rivers (the Sacandaga can be seen entering the Hudson from the right). At the far end of the bridge, a small footpath leads down to the river. There is not much picnicking space, but it is a good opportunity to scramble on the rocks along the Hudson and feel the power of the river as it flows by.

Crossing the bridge, you are entering the town of Hadley, with its prominent sign "Home of New York State's Dude Ranch Trail." Hadley is a smaller and less elegant town than Luzerne. If you wish to explore the downtown, continue straight ahead a few tenths of a mile, then return to the turn for Stony Creek.

12.7 At the Hadley General Store, turn right onto County Road 1, following the arrow to Stony Creek.

If you are low on water, you will want to fill up at the store, as

Rockwell Falls, in the town of Lake Luzerne

93

there is no other opportunity to do so for the next 20 miles.

As you ride along County Road 1, the surroundings again change. The mixed deciduous forest shifts to primarily piney woods. The shoulder shrinks, though it is still fairly usable, and there is much less traffic as you proceed north out of town. The road more or less follows a railroad track and the Hudson, though the river is rarely visible from this part of the tour. Homes are less likely to be summer residences, and more typical of the housing in much of the Adirondack Park. This kind of road is what is generally referred to as the "real" Adirondacks: rural, quiet, and beautiful.

15.7 *Note the railroad crossing, which cuts across the road at a steep angle. The terrain is gently rolling through this area.*

18.9 *Begin a climb up a hill that is steeper than it looks and thankfully short.*

19.3 *Top of the hill.*

The welcoming sign for Stony Creek declares "The Road to a Friendly Town Is Never Long." This is true, but this tour won't be going all the way into Stony Creek. (See Tour 16, which begins and ends at the four corners of Stony Creek.)

20.8 *At the gun shop, clearly marked "GUNS" in 3-foot letters, turn right onto Grist Mill Road. The road is very steep, often sandy, with poor pavement; descend with caution.*

21.1 *Just after crossing over Stony Creek, turn right and begin a delightful, gentle, long downhill along the creek.*

23.0 *Stony Creek veers away from the road to join the Hudson River.*

The Hudson is visible again at this point. The river is wider, deeper, and smooth, in contrast to the rocky falls of Lake Luzerne. As you ride, note the sandy "sidewalk" on the left side of the road; it is used by horses from the nearby ranches.

24.2 *On the right, the 1000 Acres Ranch is one of the remaining working dude ranches in the area. The railroad is again visible along the right side of the road.*

25.9 *At the top of a small rise, enter the town of Thurman.*

The road becomes increasingly hilly at this point, with a few short, steep climbs and descents.

28.0 Begin ascending the steepest hill on this part of the tour.

Half a mile later, at the top, note the biker's favorite sign: a truck descending a hill with "Use Low Gear" posted beneath it!

29.0 In the village of Thurman Station, follow the road to the right, as it becomes County Road 418. Directly after the turn, you will cross a rough set of railroad tracks.

29.2 Cross the Hudson River again.

The road winds along the Schroon River for the next couple of miles, and as it enters Warrensburg, the traffic will begin to increase.

30.5 Note the old sawmill to the left.

This was the Warrensburg Board and Paper Company, long fallen into disuse. From here, the river is winding and lazy, and there are often children and adults fishing from its banks.

32.0 Herrick Variety Store (established in 1893) offers the first opportunity to fill up water bottles since Hadley.

32.2 The Grist Mill Restaurant is on the left.

The Grist Mill is located in the old mill building, overlooking the Schroon. It contains numerous grindstones, chutes, barrels, and cogs from the original mill. The restaurant is only open for dinner and is quite expensive, but if it is open you may get a chance to go inside to look at the mill artifacts. (For dinner, you will want to ask directions to Anthony's Ristorante Italiano, on the outskirts of Warrensburg—it is to carbo-loading what the Vatican is to prayer.)

32.3 Turn left at the stop sign, crossing the Schroon River one more time. Directly after the bridge, turn right onto Water Street.

On Water Street you may have to wait for a few moments for the flock of ducks and geese that congregate near the bridge to move off the road before you can proceed.

32.6 Turn right at the stoplight onto Main Street, which is US 9.

The Brew and Stew Restaurant, at the corner, is a good place for a basic meal. Frances Antiques, on your left after the turn, is the oldest building in Warrensburg. It was built as a blacksmith shop in the early 1800s.

US 9 carries a great deal of traffic, including large trucks, through Warrensburg, but most of it will turn off onto I-87 just half a mile ahead, leaving the remaining road open for bikers.

33.2 **Continue straight on US 9 past the turn for I-87.**

This is the last uphill on the route, and there is an excellent shoulder. As you climb, you will hear the traffic on the nearby Northway speeding by, but the traffic on US 9 will be quite light.

34.5 **The top of the hill gives way to a 3-mile downhill into the village of Lake George. The buildings along the road will increase as you approach the village.**

37.9 **Junction of US 9 and NY 9N. Continue on US 9.**

Traffic will pick up dramatically, especially in the summer months, as you enter Lake George's business district.

38.2 **Return to the Old Warren County Courthouse.**

14

Bolton Landing: Lake and River Ride

Distance: 32 miles
Terrain: Moderate, with a 3-mile series of steep climbs

This ride moves north along the shore of Lake George, taking in some lovely views of the lake, before turning inland at Bolton Landing and following the Schroon River south. Because much of the ride is on the main road leaving Lake George Village, this ride would be most enjoyable off-season or on a summer weekday when the traffic is not too heavy.

The terrain on this route is rolling except for a 3-mile series of fairly steep climbs out of the Lake George valley. With frequent rests, they should be possible for the average bicyclist. Twenty-second pauses are the most beneficial; these "granny stops" allow your muscles to flush out lactic acid, but aren't long enough for your muscles to become tight and cold.

0.0   Begin at the Old Warren County Courthouse at the corner of Canada and Amherst Streets. Ride north on Canada Street (US 9), keeping the lake on your right.

0.4   Bear right onto NY 9N.

   NY 9N travels along the shore of Lake George. While this can be a busy road, a small shoulder gives adequate space for single-file riding. Note the many estates, old manors, hotels, and cabins nestled between the road and the lake, and the many glimpses of the lake itself. Pull into the parking lots of the hotels for a better view. The terrain along this stretch is rolling, but never steep.

3.5   Enter the village of Diamond Point.

4.3   Note the Diamond Point Community Church on your left, with its fine stone architecture.

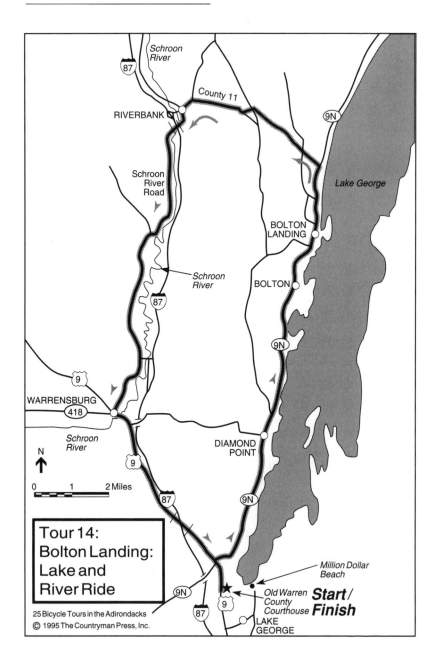

Schroon River

87

County 11

RIVERBANK

9N

Schroon River Road

Lake George

BOLTON LANDING

Schroon River

87

BOLTON

9N

9

WARRENSBURG

418

Schroon River

DIAMOND POINT

N

0   1   2 Miles

9

87

9N

**Tour 14:
Bolton Landing:
Lake and
River Ride**

25 Bicycle Tours in the Adirondacks
© 1995 The Countryman Press, Inc.

Million Dollar Beach

9N

87

9

Old Warren County Courthouse

**Start /
Finish**

LAKE GEORGE

4.6   *As you pass the sign indicating that you have entered the town of Bolton, the terrain becomes increasingly hilly.*

8.3   *Note the Bolton Landing Cemetery on the right.*

9.2   *Enter the town of Bolton Landing.*

This town was the first European settlement on Lake George, and the first resort hotel in the area, the Mohican House, was built here in 1800 (it has since become a private residence). The town still has a historic feel about it, with stone walls and wrought iron fences bordering many of the properties along the road. Though tourism is obviously the major industry here, Bolton Landing has none of the frenetic pace of Lake George; elegance and tradition are the rule. There are many beautiful homes and estates along the way, and upscale shops.

Bolton Landing is home to the Marcella Sembrich Memorial Studio, an opera museum. Marcella Sembrich was a European opera singer who joined the Metropolitan Opera in 1898, and she made her home in this building from 1921 to 1935, often bringing students to stay with her during the summer months. The studio offers concerts throughout the summer.

9.8   *The Church of St. Sacrement, Episcopal, is on the left.*

This church has an interesting wooden bell tower built apart from the church building itself. Saint Isaac Jogues, a Jesuit missionary, was the first European known to have seen Lake George. He named it Lac du St. Sacrement, and the name lives on in this Episcopal church.

10.0   *A visitors information center and the Bolton Historical Museum are housed in a former Catholic church on your right.*

10.5   *Veteran's Park and the Bolton Landing public beach are on your right.*

Take an opportunity to get off the bike and walk along the water for a while. Just past the park, the road rises more steeply as it leaves Bolton Landing.

11.5   *At the top of the hill, the Candlelight Motel and Cottages offer a spectacular view of the lake from their parking lot; it's worth stopping for a look.*

11.9 Turn left on County Road 11, toward the town of Riverbank.

The steepest hill of the ride begins here, and it is also quite long. As you stop to rest along the way, be sure to look back over your shoulder at Lake George, which opens up into a beautiful vista the farther you climb.

12.7 You made it to the top of this climb.

Take one more look back at the lake. Don't despair at the sight of another sizable hill just before you; it's much shorter than the last one. As you ride, note the views north (to the right) along the Lake George valley, with its undulating mountaintops. In the fall, when the trees are turning, this is a spectacular spot.

13.8 You've reached the top of the second climb. Only one more climb to go!

14.2 Begin the last significant uphill of the route.

14.7 That's it! You made it!

At the top of this hill, you are rewarded with a terrific view of the Adirondack mountains stretching out before you to the west. Take a moment to drink in the shapes and colors of the mountains before you begin a dazzling descent to the Schroon River valley.

16.6 At the bottom of the hill, the bridge crossing the Schroon River is steel.

Ride across it slowly and carefully, or, better yet, dismount and walk across, particularly if the bridge might be wet.

16.8 Turn left onto Schroon River Road.

This 8-mile stretch of the ride is fairly flat, with little traffic (most of which takes the nearby Northway). It follows the Schroon River south through lovely wooded areas, broken by homes and small fields, several of which are horse pastures. The woods vary between deciduous and piney areas; note how the pine woods hold cool air, even at midday.

25.3 The Warrensburg Central School is on the right, and the road descends quite steeply to US 9 in Warrensburg.

25.8 Turn left at the stoplight to travel south on US 9.

Note the Stewarts (public bathrooms and basic munchies) on your right before you turn. Across the street to the left, the Brew and Stew offers simple, good pub food.

Frances Antiques, on your left after the turn, is the oldest building in Warrensburg. It was built as a blacksmith shop in the early 1800s.

US 9 carries a great deal of traffic, including large trucks, through Warrensburg, but most of it will turn onto I-87 just 0.5 mile ahead, leaving the remaining route open for bikers.

27.0 Continue straight on US 9 past the turn for I-87.

This last uphill is not steep, and there is an excellent shoulder. As you climb, you will hear the traffic on the nearby Northway speeding by, but the traffic on US 9 will be quite light.

28.3 Roll past the top of the hill.

It gives way to a 3-mile downhill into the village of Lake George. The number of buildings along the road will increase as you approach the village.

31.7 Junction of US 9 and NY 9N. Continue on US 9.

Traffic will pick up dramatically, especially in the summer months, as you enter Lake George's business district.

32.0 Return to the Old Warren County Courthouse.

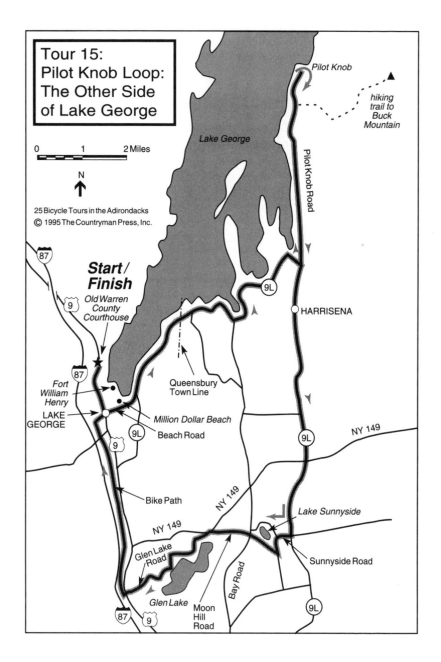

Tour 15:
Pilot Knob Loop:
The Other Side
of Lake George

Pilot Knob

hiking
trail to
Buck
Mountain

Lake George

Pilot Knob Road

0   1   2 Miles

N

25 Bicycle Tours in the Adirondacks
© 1995 The Countryman Press, Inc.

87

9L

Start /
Finish

9

*Old Warren
County
Courthouse*

HARRISENA

87

*Fort
William
Henry*

*Queensbury
Town Line*

LAKE
GEORGE

9L

Million Dollar Beach

9

Beach Road

9L

NY 149

Bike Path

NY 149

Lake Sunnyside

NY 149

Glen Lake
Road

Bay Road

Sunnyside Road

87

9

Glen Lake

Moon
Hill
Road

9L

102

15
Pilot Knob Loop:
The Other Side of Lake George

Distance: *31.3 miles*
Terrain: *Easy to moderate*

This ride is the easiest of the Lake George–based loops, and is perhaps the least trafficked. It offers three distinct views of the area: the less traveled and less kitschy east shore of Lake George; the bogs, woods, and dignified old farms of northern Queensbury; and a portion of a delightful bike trail that runs through the woods between Glens Falls and Lake George. The terrain is flat to rolly, with no major grades on the ride.

This is the only ride in the book that is not entirely within the "blue line" of the Adirondack Park; it may be interesting for you to notice the differences in development patterns on either side of the boundary. Please note: The mileage readings on the bike-path portion of this ride are only approximate—they could not be double-checked with a car's odometer.

0.0 *Start loop heading south on US 9 with the Old Warren County Courthouse on your left.*

0.2 *Turn left onto Beach Road (a continuation of McGillis Avenue).*
The far south end of Lake George is home to the remnants of the tourist shops that line US 9. Watch for pedestrians stepping out into the road.

0.4 *Pass by Fort William Henry on your right and a surprisingly dignified collection of paddle-wheeled tourist steamships on the docks to your left.*

0.7 *Veer right as Beach Road divides through Lake George public*

beach and park. The beach is also known as Million Dollar Beach, which recalls a tonier era, when it was the playground of the rich and famous.

1.2 *Pump your way up a very steep, but only 100-yard-long, hill.*

1.3 *Turn left onto NY 9L.*

1.4 *Pass Usher Park on your left.*

This area of Lake George is upscale residential, the terrain is rolling, there is little shoulder on the road, but also little traffic. Enjoy the glimpses of the lake to your left.

3.4 *Cross the Queensbury town line.*

5.2 *Notice the bog on your right and Dunham Bay Boat Shop on your left.*

5.5 *Begin a 0.5-mile climb. The road cuts and curves dramatically through the native rock.*

6.9 *Pass the Cleverdale Country Store.*

7.7 *Turn left onto Pilot Knob Road.*

This portion of the ride is more wooded and rural as you travel north along the east shore of the lake. The terrain is rolling.

8.4 *Cross the Washington County line.*

9.9 *Pass the very cute Kattskills Post Office.*

11.0 *Notice the trailhead to Buck Mountain Summit, a 3.3-mile hike.*

11.6 *You are passing through the grounds of the Chingagchook YMCA.*

11.8 *You've reached the end of the road at the small public beach.*

Across Lake George you can see Cat Mountain. Perhaps you can spy one of the steamboats plying the water. To continue the loop, turn around and return to NY 9L.

16.0 *Turn left on NY 9L.*

16.1 *You may wish to stop at the tiny Williamson Grocery for a drink or a snack.*

The terrain becomes quite flat for several miles.

16.9 *On the right is a 19th-century church converted into a private home.*

17.6 *Enter the hamlet of Harrisena.*

18.7 *The wooded landscape opens to small farming fields, beautiful old brick farmhouses and scrubby bogs.*

20.6 *Cross NY 149.*

There is a Stewarts convenience store on the right. After the intersection there is a moderate hill. The terrain becomes rolling again.

21.4 *As you cross the Lake George town line, you leave the Adirondack Park.*

22.2 *Turn right onto Sunnyside Road.*

22.6 *Pass by tiny Lake Sunnyside on the right. There is an old cemetery on the left.*

23.2 *Cross Bay Road. Sunnyside Road becomes the Moon Hill Road. Continue straight.*

23.4 *Enjoy a short, dramatic curve downhill.*

Looking north on Lake George, with its historic paddle-wheel steamboats

There are a few short, steep rollers along this stretch of Moon Hill.

24.5 Moon Hill Road becomes Glen Lake Road as you come into view of Glen Lake.

25.8 Turn right onto the bike path and return to Lake George.

This delightful bike path parallels US 9 back to Lake George. US 9 is seriously unpleasant for bicyclists between Glens Falls and Lake George, given over to strip malls and horrendous traffic even on weekdays. In contrast, the bike path meanders through some lovely woods and fields.

At around mile 26.7, the bike path crosses a wooden bridge over NY 149. If you need the services of a bike shop at this point, climb off the path to the left before going over the bridge and proceed west about 200 yards to Syd and Dusty's Outfitters.

At around mile 28.4, the path comes out of the woods to run along US 9 for 0.25 mile, affording a view of Magic Forest's giant Uncle Sam silently beckoning the tourists. Fortunately, you quickly duck back into the woods.

The bike path ends at Beach Road in the Lake George public beach and park.

29.6 Turn left on Beach Road back toward the village.

31.1 Turn right at intersection with US 9.

31.3 Arrive back at courthouse.

16
Thurman and Stony Creek: Hilly Backwaters

Distance: 18 miles
Terrain: Relatively easy, with one sustained hill, and pavement that would benefit from knobby tires

On those busy summer weekends when much of the rest of the park is a riot of people and traffic, or on those foliage weekends in the fall when the tour buses swarm the High Peaks, this is one corner of the Adirondacks where peace can be all but guaranteed. We last biked this route on a brilliantly blue Saturday morning of Memorial Day weekend in 1994, and were passed by perhaps a dozen cars the whole time.

The loneliness is paradoxical in a sense, since Stony Creek and Thurman lie in the southeast portion of the park, near the Northway and closer to flatland civilization than most other regions. But the scenery tends more to steep wooded hills than the massive granite outcrops beloved of calendar-makers and climbers—most of the relatively small number of summer people have been coming here for years and even generations, often to one of the dude ranches that still exist in the area. And then there is the terrain: Those who have spent time in West Virginia will find Stony Creek reminiscent, for it is set in a creek-bottom hollow, a place from which there is no direct route in or out.

Once the population of Stony Creek was considerably higher than its current 666—the abundant supply of running water powered sawmills and helped float logs out of the Adirondacks to market, and the profusion of hemlocks supported a tanning industry. Adirondack historian Barbara McMartin notes that fires following heavy lumbering made the forest much less productive, and even cut the flow of water from the denuded forest, but the community has hung on. (Its independence be-

107

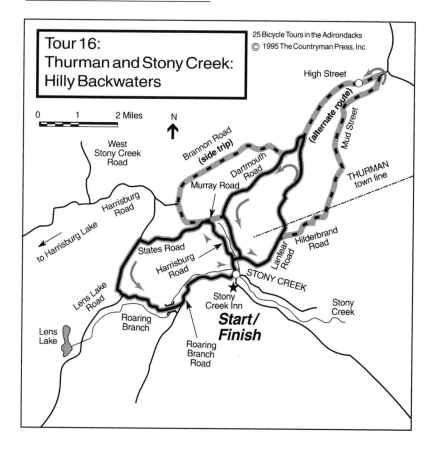

Tour 16:
Thurman and Stony Creek:
Hilly Backwaters

25 Bicycle Tours in the Adirondacks
© 1995 The Countryman Press, Inc.

came loudly clear in the early 1990s when it successfully fought off a county plan to take the trash from the city of Glens Falls and dump it in this out-of-the-way place.)

Along with the lovely shaded roads navigated by this tour, Stony Creek provides access to the Wilcox Lake Wild Forest, one of the park's many large protected areas. A look at the map demonstrates that the core of the state holdings in the Adirondacks really begins on the western edge of Stony Creek, land that is easily accessible by car or, better yet, mountain bike. And since the public land is officially designated wild forest and not wilderness, there is no rule preventing pedal trips through this lovely land.

0.0 *This trip begins and ends at the one small cluster of commerce in the entire area, the four corners in downtown Stony Creek.*

There are two small grocery and dry-goods stores (one of which goes by the delightful name of Floyd's Mall, and then there is the Stony Creek Inn, the real center of the town's cultural life. "Inn" should not bring to mind images of some quaint bed & breakfast with ruffled skirts around the sinks—this place is more closely related to a roadhouse, as evidenced by the big dance floor next to the bar. It really swings on Sundays, when Mexican food is served and bluegrass pounds out from the bandstand, but the food is basic and good anytime, and the draft beer is cold. But that's still 18 hilly miles away.

From the inn's parking lot, head northwest on the Harrisburg Road, passing the library, the Methodist church, and the volunteer fire company.

0.3 *Turn right on Lanfear Road, by a pretty park with picnic tables and playground equipment that borders rushing Stony Creek.*

0.5 *Continue straight on Lanfear, ignoring the main turn to the left.*

You will stay on Lanfear for almost 5 miles, mainly climbing on a series of gentle-to-rigorous hills, all of them short. As you pedal, you can notice the results of recent logging in many places, chiefly a thinned-out forest with skinnier trees.

2.1 *Pass Hildenbrandt Road on the right, a pleasant dirt track that mountain bikes can follow. (You can extend the ride by a few miles by taking Hildenbrandt, which becomes Mud Street when it crosses the Thurman town line, to the intersection with High Street, where you can turn left and eventually intersect this route at the 4.9-mile mark.)*

4.9 *Turn left onto Dartmouth Road at the stop sign, and then pass through a short and lovely agricultural section that looks nearly Vermontlike with its stony fields.*

A barn on the left at 5.5 miles, still intact and in use, gives silent testimony to the construction ability of earlier settlers.

5.6 Pass Brannon Road on the right, a long and fairly bumpy and rutted dirt logger's road that would serve as a decent side trip. It eventually connects to Harrisburg Road just west of the 10.7-mile point on this trip.

8.1 Near the bottom of a long descent, stay on the main road where it intersects with Murray Road. Caution: The sign says 10 miles per hour is a safe speed to take this turn, but that's fast on a bike—especially in the springtime, when there's still a winter's worth of road sand along the margins of the pavement.

9.2 Turn right on Lanfear Road, again crossing Stony Creek—this 0.2 mile is the knot in this figure-eight loop, the only repeating section of this trip.

9.4 Turn right on the Harrisburg Road, heading out from town.

Speeding through Stony Creek

10.7 Turn left onto States Road, and begin a long climb that—with only a few level patches—continues for the next 1.5 miles.

If instead of turning onto States Road, you continued to ride out on Harrisburg Road, you would eventually reach Harrisburg Lake—or by turning on West Stony Creek Road come to the hub of trails radiating out from Baldwin Springs. But the farther parts of these treks are possible only on a mountain bike, and be warned that you have left civilization behind and the only way to return to it is to retreat.

12.3 Note the cemetery tucked back in the woods.

12.6 Stay on the main branch of States Road, uphill and to the left.

14.1 From about this point you commence a lengthy and occasionally steep downhill that will take you much of the way back to Stony Creek. The pavement is not uniformly good, so be sure to keep your speed in check.

14.4 Note the road on the right to Lens Lake.

If you are looking for a picnic spot, this would be hard to beat. Lens Lake is about 2 miles uphill on a decent road, and it offers a rare example of a quaking bog. It is most easily explored with a canoe, and it's a little too quaking to really walk out on, but as a sight it is one of nature's most curious. A mat of sphagnum—6 feet deep in places—covers most of the northern end of this body of water, and water lilies cover much of the rest. McMartin notes the presence of pitcher plants, cranberries and sweet gale, bladderworts, Labrador tea, and swamp laurel, as well as carnivorous sundews.

16.5 Another lunch spot, the steel deck over Roaring Branch, a rushing mountain brook that pushes down to Stony Creek. (There's another such bridge 0.7 mile farther along.)

18.0 Back to the Stony Creek Inn—and also Genny, the local beer, on tap.

NORTH CREEK ROUTES

North Creek Routes: Teddy's Trail, Minerva–Olmstedville Loop, Speculator, The Lakes of Chester, and White-water Challenge

The hamlet of North Creek, located within the town of Johnsburg, is the center for five tours reaching in different directions. Like many towns in the area, North Creek began as a logging settlement in the mid-1800s; loggers, floating timber down the Hudson River, discovered a good site for their camps at the "north creek," which flows into the Hudson. Not many years later, a tannery was built in the town, drawing on the ample supply of hemlock bark from the surrounding forest to provide the tannin for curing leathers. At about this time, the Adirondack Railroad was built through North Creek, bringing in supplies and hides to be cured, and shipping out the finished products.

As logging and tanning declined, Henry Hudson Barton began mining garnet on nearby Gore Mountain for use as a commercial abrasive. Garnet fever swept through North Creek, and for a time several mines were in operation, extracting the "Adirondack ruby" from the earth. While most of these mines are closed today, Barton Mines is still in operation. Garnet was and is so plentiful in the area that garnet crystals can often be found in the rocks of North Creek and neighboring North River, particularly in locally produced gravel and crushed stone used in driveways and along the roads.

North Creek entered the annals of United States history in 1901, when then Vice-President Theodore Roosevelt, hiking 40 miles away on Mt. Marcy, the highest peak in New York State, was told by messenger that President McKinley had been shot. Roosevelt made a long, hazardous dash back to civilization, and upon arriving at North Creek on September 14, was told that the president had died. Roosevelt took the presidential oath of office at the train station before traveling back to Washington.

Less than half a century later, in the wake of the 1932 Winter Olympics at Lake Placid, North Creek again achieved national recognition, this time as a premier ski resort. A group of local residents, inspired by the Winter Games, cut trails on and around Gore Mountain, and skiers began to flock to them. In the 1930s and 1940s, tourists from New York City traveled to North Creek by train to spend the weekend skiing at Gore. A train would leave New York City at midnight on a Friday and pull into North Creek just after seven o'clock Saturday morning. There would be two mad days of skiing, and then a return trip to the city late at night. In the 1960s, the current Gore Mountain Ski Center opened, and it has been operating ever since, drawing skiers from around the Northeast throughout the winter months. There are currently plans to revive the ski trains from New York City.

The skiing industry has created a demand for lodging in the area, and there is no shortage of places to stay in North Creek. There are no campgrounds in the immediate area, and accommodations range from basic motels to the four-star Copperfield Inn. A favorite is the Goose Pond Inn Bed & Breakfast, where Beverly and Jim Englert will welcome you in for the night and send you off in the morning with a fantastic breakfast (518-251-3434).

All four of these tours begin and end at the North Creek Deli and Marketplace. A more modern version of the old-time general store, the North Creek Deli offers everything from thermal underwear to espresso, penny candy (well, nickel and quarter candy) to hiking boots, and souvenir T-shirts to locally crafted birdhouses. Owners John and Noelle Harvey sell homemade breads, cookies, and muffins, as well as generously loaded submarine sandwiches. The Deli is a good place to snack before and after your ride and get to meet the local inhabitants of North Creek.

Bike Shops

The Mountain & Boardertown
Main Street, North Creek
full repair shop

Kindred Spirits Outfitters
Olmstedville
bike rentals, emergency repairs

17
Teddy's Trail:
Indian Lake, Long Lake, and Newcomb

Distance: *79.9 miles*
Terrain: *Rolling to hilly, with a couple of very memorable climbs and descents that can be difficult, but not impossible for the average rider*

This tour can be ridden in 1 long, hard day, or broken up into 2 or 3 moderate days with more time to browse, hike, canoe, and explore the towns along the way.

0.0 *Begin riding west at the North Creek Deli and Marketplace, with the Deli on your right. As you move out of town, note the Hudson River on your right, and the sawmill, which is still in operation along the river.*

0.6 *Turn right onto NY 28.*

A generous shoulder along much of this ride diminishes the effects of the traffic, much of it trucks, along the route. For the next 5 miles, you will ride within view of the Hudson River. The river's character varies with the seasons; in the spring and early summer, the water is high and fast, and as the summer and fall progress the water level falls so that in places rocks can be seen all the way across the water. It looks as though one could walk across, but if you try, be careful—there are hidden deep pockets with fast-moving water. A wading stick is helpful.

2.5 *Watch the railroad tracks, which cross NY 28 here at quite a steep angle.*

These tracks are a continuation of the railroad that extended from New York City to North Creek; they travel on to the old iron ore

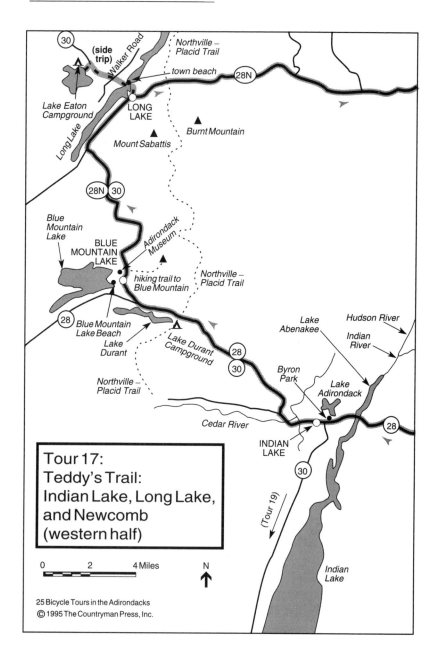

30
(side trip)
Walker Road
Northville – Placid Trail

town beach
28N

Lake Eaton Campground

LONG LAKE

Long Lake

Burnt Mountain

Mount Sabattis

28N 30

Blue Mountain Lake

BLUE MOUNTAIN LAKE

Adirondack Museum

hiking trail to Blue Mountain

Northville – Placid Trail

28

Blue Mountain Lake Beach
Lake Durant

Lake Durant Campground

Northville – Placid Trail

Lake Abenakee

Hudson River

Indian River

28

Byron Park

28
30

Lake Adirondack

Cedar River

INDIAN LAKE

30

(Tour 19)

28

**Tour 17:
Teddy's Trail:
Indian Lake, Long Lake,
and Newcomb
(western half)**

0   2   4 Miles

N

Indian Lake

25 Bicycle Tours in the Adirondacks
© 1995 The Countryman Press, Inc.

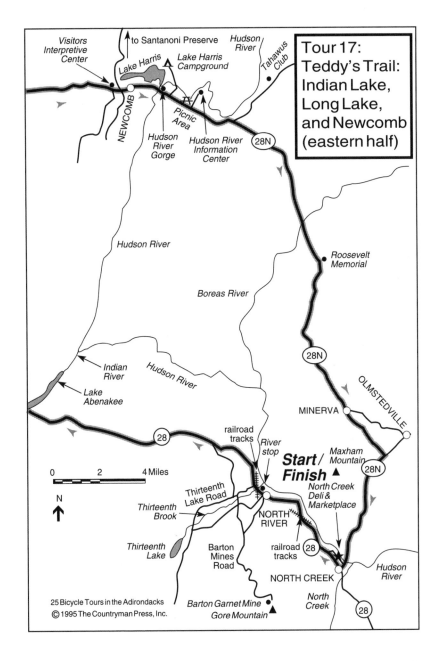

Tour 17:
Teddy's Trail:
Indian Lake,
Long Lake,
and Newcomb
(eastern half)

Visitors Interpretive Center

to Santanoni Preserve

Hudson River

Tahawus Club

Lake Harris

NEWCOMB

Lake Harris Campground

Picnic Area

Hudson River Gorge

Hudson River Information Center

28N

Hudson River

Roosevelt Memorial

Boreas River

Indian River

Hudson River

Lake Abenakee

28

railroad tracks

River stop

MINERVA

OLMSTEDVILLE

Start / Finish ▲

Maxham Mountain

28N

Thirteenth Lake Road

Thirteenth Brook

NORTH RIVER

North Creek Deli & Marketplace

Thirteenth Lake

Barton Mines Road

railroad tracks

28

NORTH CREEK

Hudson River

0   2   4 Miles

N

25 Bicycle Tours in the Adirondacks
© 1995 The Countryman Press, Inc.

Barton Garnet Mine
Gore Mountain ▲

North Creek

28

and titanium mine at Tahawus. To your right is a parking area, one of several along this stretch of the route.

4.2   *Enter the town of North River.*

4.4   *Whitewater Challengers, on the left, is one of the best of the many local white-water rafting and kayaking companies that lead tours on the Hudson and other nearby rivers.*

4.5   *Barton Mines Road is on the left.*

This road leads to the still-operating garnet mine of the area. Shaw's General Store, located at the intersection, carries basic foods, fishing gear, and maps of the area. Jasco Minerals, across from Shaw's, has a large collection of rocks, minerals, and fossils, and specializes in native garnet jewelry.

5.1   *Note the parking area on the right, which spans Thirteenth Brook as it joins the Hudson River.*

This is an excellent place to scramble along the rocks or watch the fly-fisherfolk seeking trout in the Hudson's chilly waters. The road to your left leads uphill along Thirteenth Brook to the rest of the hamlet of North River, to Thirteenth Lake, and finally up a dirt road to Garnet Hill Lodge, a former Adirondack Great Camp that is now a four-season resort with an excellent cross-country skiing course and a terrific restaurant (518-251-2220).

5.5   *The railroad tracks again cross NY 28 at a steep angle. The tracks continue to follow the Hudson River north, as the road pulls away to the west, toward Indian Lake.*

5.8   *You will begin climbing a series of hills as you leave the Hudson.*

None of these climbs is particularly steep, though this first is nearly 2 miles long. As you climb, New York State "Bike Route" signs will cheer you along to the top, assuring you that other bikers have come this way and survived.

7.4   *Top of the first hill.*

8.4   *Note the giant chairs on your right, the advertising for Rustic Furniture, which is made here.*

8.8   *Begin the last rise on this series of hills.*

9.5 *This is the top of the climb from North River.*

Now that you're at the top of the ridge, you'll find bogs, meandering streams, and beaver dams along both sides of the road. The woods contain more pine, and are delightfully cool on summer days. The road will continue to be rolling, with smaller hills as you journey west.

13.9 *Note the view to the left of some of the striking peaks of the Siamese Ponds Wilderness Area, most notably Bullhead Mountain.*

14.2 *Begin a steep 0.5-mile descent as you pass the sign for Indian Lake.*

16.0 *Cross Lake Abenakee.*

This is the northernmost body of water connected to Indian Lake, which extends some 12 miles to the south-southwest. The town of Indian Lake claims status as the "Whitewater Capital of the Adirondacks," with good reason. Daily throughout the spring, summer, and fall, the Lake Abenakee dam is opened on its northern end and the water flows into the Indian River. White-water rafters, kayakers, and canoers ride the crest of the flow down the Indian and into the Hudson River, traveling as far south as the town of North River. During the spring runoff, when water levels in the Hudson often exceed 10 feet, the white water is fantastic.

To your left, a parking area on Lake Abenakee provides a good place to stop and enjoy the view. As you leave the lake, you will begin climbing a series of short but steep hills into the hamlet of Indian Lake.

16.9 *Lake Adirondack lies on your right, with Byron Park just on the other side of the bridge.*

17.4 *At the junction of NY 28 and NY 30, continue straight.*

A Grand Union grocery store is on your right. For a worthwhile lunch, stop at Angelina's Pizza on your left, which offers some of the best pizza in the area. The *pollo*, a pizza with chicken, sun-dried tomatoes, and pesto, is a house specialty.

At this intersection, Tour 19, the Speculator loop along the Sacandaga, splits off to the south.

19.2 As you leave the hamlet of Indian Lake, you cross Cedar River, which flows north from the Moose River Wilderness.

The broad shoulder that has graced NY 28 since North Creek narrows somewhat, but is still quite adequate for riding well out of the way of traffic. You will pass several trailheads, marking the trails to local lakes and ponds. The road rolls uphill and down for the next several miles.

24.0 Enter the town of Blue Mountain Lake; the sign is on the left.

25.8 The access road to the Lake Durant Public Campground and Day-Use Area is to the left.

This is a fine, state-run campground on the shore of Lake Durant, which makes an excellent place to stay if you wish to do this route in 3 days.

26.2 The Northville–Placid Trail crosses NY 28.

This wilderness hiking trail covers 133 miles from Northville, on the northern shore of the Sacandaga Lake, to the High Peaks region and Lake Placid. You will cross the trail again between Long Lake and Newcomb.

27.8 Enter the hamlet of Blue Mountain Lake.

28.7 NY 30 and NY 28 divide; turn right to follow NY 30 north (which is also NY 28N at this point, which should not be confused with NY 28!).

The Blue Mountain Lake Service Center, on your left at the intersection, carries basic supplies. Potter's Restaurant, directly across NY 30, serves a good breakfast, lunch, or dinner in an Adirondack setting.

(If you wish to explore the "downtown" of Blue Mountain Lake, turn left onto NY 28 and ride 0.5 mile into town. The public beach offers a cooling dip as well as a nice view of Blue Mountain Lake with Blue Mountain towering to the north. The Adirondack Lakes Center for the Arts, on the left as you ride through town, contains exhibitions of traditional Adirondack crafts, contemporary art, and a small gift shop. ALCA offers weekday and weekend courses for children and adults in dance, local crafts, photography, and Adirondack storytelling.)

29.0 *Back on NY 30, Blue Mountain Designs, on the right, sells a wide selection of products by traditional and modern artists.*

At this point you will begin to climb the steepest hill of the route, a 1-mile ascent over the shoulder of Blue Mountain.

29.8 *On the left is the Adirondack Museum, described by the* **New York Times** *as "the best museum of its kind in the world."*

Overlooking Blue Mountain Lake, the museum offers an unparalleled glimpse into the world of the Adirondacks. Films, paintings, photos, wooden Adirondack guideboats, rustic furniture, and a railroad car each tell its piece of Adirondack history. The museum is definitely worth several hours of browsing time, and you will come away with a richer understanding of the Adirondack Park and its inhabitants. Or, if nothing else, pause in the parking lot to catch your breath, admire the view, and gather your strength for the last 0.25-mile uphill.

30.1 *At the top of the hill, the 2-mile trail to the top of Blue Mountain begins to the right of the road.*

A lookout tower at the top of the mountain offers magnificent views of the Adirondacks in all directions. As you come over the crest of the hill, a delightful, long descent awaits you; the road continues to roll between here and Long Lake, but the hills are much more gentle.

36.1 *Enter the town of Long Lake.*

Note the mama bear and cub on the town sign. You will just begin to see the lake to the left, and motels and cottages cluster along the road together with private homes. Long Lake is well named: It is nearly 12 miles long, and only a mile wide at the broadest point.

39.4 *As you come into the hamlet of Long Lake, NY 30 and NY 28N split.*

Follow NY 28N to the right to continue on the bike tour toward Newcomb. This part of NY 28N is designated the Roosevelt–Marcy Highway to commemorate Teddy Roosevelt's hurried trip from the High Peaks, north of Newcomb, to North Creek after President McKinley's assassination.

Hoss's Country Corner, on the corner of NY 30 and NY 28N, is a modern version of the traditional general store, with camping supplies, gourmet jams and jellies, books, maps, and food.

If you wish to explore Long Lake, the rest of the town lies along NY 30 to the left. Following the road through town, you will come to Northern Borne Supermarket, another general store stocking food and supplies, which caters to a more local clientele. The handsome old Adirondack Hotel rises to your left. At the town beach, you can hire a seaplane for a ride over the mountains or catch a bite to eat at the Island Snackbar.

If you are planning to split this route into two even sections, or if you wish to ride it in 3 days, you will probably want to stay in or near Long Lake, which is the halfway point of the tour (though most of the uphill riding is over). Lake Eaton Campground, 2 miles west on NY 30, offers fine camping at a state-run facility. For more luxurious lodging, try the Mountain View Farm of Long Lake, a bed & breakfast at the intersection of Walker Road and Adams Park Drive, which features spun wool from sheep raised on the farm (518-624-2521).

40.1 *Continuing east on NY 28N, note the beaver dam to the right of the road.*

The next 0.25-mile offers views of Mt. Sabattis and Burnt Mountain.

40.9 *The Northville–Placid Trail crosses NY 28N on its way north.*

As you continue on NY 28N to Newcomb, you get a feel for the wilderness of the Adirondack Park—there are few houses or other sign of human habitation for the next 10 miles. Only the occasional stream or pond breaks the presence of the woods on either side of the highway. It is not unusual to see deer along the highway for the next 30 miles.

52.1 *Note on your left the sign for the visitors interpretive center, just north of NY 28N. Here you will find displays describing the natural history of the area, as well as weekend classes in local crafts, from fly-tying to taxidermy.*

52.4 *Enter the town of Newcomb. "Heart of the Adirondacks," the sign into town proclaims, and indeed, Newcomb is the town closest to the geographic center of the Adirondack Park.*

53.2 *Note to the left the sign to Santanoni Preserve.*

This former Great Camp hosted such dignitaries as Theodore Roosevelt in its heyday. Santanoni's 12,000 acres have since been acquired by the state of New York, and the buildings and land are a destination for hikers, mountain bikers, and cross-country skiers.

53.7 *Northwoods General Store and Luncheonette, on the right, is a good place to stop for refreshments and a bathroom.*

Newcomb would surely win if an award were given for "town most scattered along a single road." Homes and small businesses span about 3 miles of NY 28N, most of them right along the highway. One gets the impression that the wilderness, not wanting to be disturbed by human habitation, has pushed the buildings right up against the road.

54.9 *As you cross the Hudson River, you are only a few miles from its source.*

Here the river appears serene and peaceful, with boggy banks; just a short distance downstream, however, it enters the Hudson River Gorge, a favorite haunt of white-water enthusiasts. The Hudson will descend some 1600 feet from this point to the Atlantic Ocean, near New York City.

The Hudson was an important route for timber drivers in the 19th and early 20th centuries. The first logs were sent down the Schroon River, which flows into the Hudson at Warrensburg, to the city of Glens Falls in 1813. Because of the remoteness of the Newcomb forests, logs felled near this area could take as long as 2 years to reach Glens Falls; they were then sent farther south to build scaffolding in New York City. By the 1950s, the demand for fresher wood by the papermaking industry, as well as a dearth of experienced log drivers, brought the log drives on the Hudson to an end.

55.3 *The access road for the Lake Harris Campground and Day-Use Area is on the left.*

56.5 *Stop here at the Newcomb Picnic Area to admire the view of the High Peaks to the north.*

Here you can see Mount Marcy, the tallest mountain in New York State; a sign at the picnic area identifies the peaks visible from this point. BBQ grills, picnic tables, and clean public washrooms make this an excellent place to stop for lunch.

To the right of the parking area, a sign directs you to the Hudson River Information Center, 0.6 mile downhill on a paved road. The center contains a history of the logging days, a spectacular view of Mount Marcy across the infant Hudson River, and maps of the area.

Across NY 28N, just behind St. Barbara's Episcopal Church, is the Winebrook Market, should you need lunch supplies.

58.4 *To the left is the road to Tahawus, an old iron mine and forge.*

A 50-foot section of the stone blast furnace still remains as silent witness to the time, 150 years ago, when Tahawus was a working forge. At first, the blast furnace removed impurities from the iron so that it could be shipped by oxcart and sled to Lake Champlain. Later, the impurities in the iron were discovered to be titanium, which was mined for its own value for several years.

The railroad that you have crossed periodically on this route runs from North Creek to end at Tahawus, and was used to ship iron and titanium south to Albany.

Tahawus is a Native American word meaning "cloud splitter";

The view of the High Peaks from the Newcomb Picnic Area

it was the native name for Mount Marcy, on whose slopes the Tahawus mine and forge rest.

63.7 *After a 0.5-mile descent, cross the Boreas River.*

This is a fine trout-fishing river that flows south to join the Hudson not far from the town of North River. As you continue down NY 28N, the terrain is rolling hills.

65.4 *On your left is a sign marking the place where Teddy Roosevelt changed horses on his trip back to North Creek from Mount Marcy.*

70.4 *Here you will note several signs warning about a very steep descent, recommending a 20 or 25 miles per hour maximum speed.*

71.2 *Enter the hamlet of Minerva.*

72.1 *Murdie's General Store is on your left.*

This is an old-fashioned general store in the traditional sense. Here you can buy snacks, fishing tackle, car parts, swimming accessories, and most anything else you might need.

72.3 *Continue straight on NY 28N as the road forks to the left around the Minerva Baptist Church.*

The road will descend for the next 2 miles.

74.7 *As you round a marsh on your right, the road to Olmstedville and Pottersville splits off to the left; stay right on NY 28N.*

The handsome mountain on the right, with the rocky face, is Maxham Mountain.

76.5 *Look out across the gravel pit on the right to Gore Mountain, which can be identified by the antenna on top and the trails cut into it.*

78.8 *A last 0.5-mile downhill brings you into North Creek once again.*

79.4 *Cross the Hudson River one more time.*

The North Creek flows into the Hudson just to the left, under the railroad bridge.

79.7 *Turn right at the stop sign onto Main Street.*

79.9 *Return to the North Creek Deli and Marketplace.*

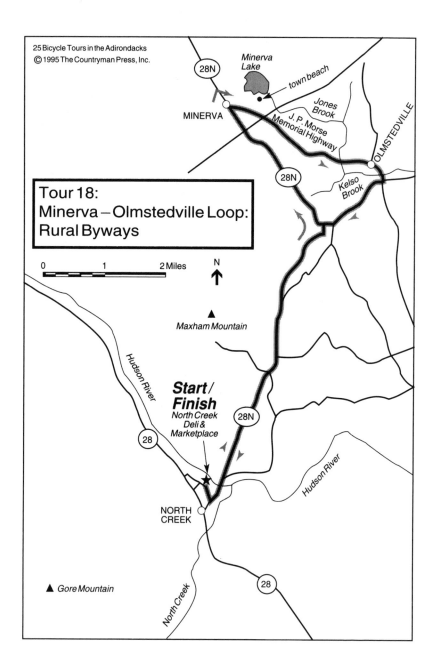

25 Bicycle Tours in the Adirondacks
© 1995 The Countryman Press, Inc.

Minerva Lake

town beach

28N

MINERVA

Jones Brook

J. P. Morse Memorial Highway

OLMSTEDVILLE

Tour 18:
Minerva – Olmstedville Loop:
Rural Byways

28N

Kelso Brook

0   1   2 Miles

N

▲
Maxham Mountain

Hudson River

***Start /
Finish***
North Creek
Deli &
Marketplace

28N

28

Hudson River

NORTH CREEK

▲ *Gore Mountain*

North Creek

28

128

18
Minerva–Olmstedville Loop: Rural Byways

Distance: *17 miles*
Terrain: *Moderately hilly*

This 1.5- to 2-hour ride makes an excellent morning or afternoon trip from North Creek.

0.0 *Leave the North Creek Deli and Marketplace, riding east (with the deli on your left) through town.*

Note Braley and Noxon Hardware on your left, which has been in business since the 1880s and has been located in its current building since 1895.

0.2 *Turn left at the stop sign onto NY 28N.*

0.5 *Cross the Hudson River.*

To the right, the North Creek flows into the Hudson under the railroad bridge; to the left, you can see the markers for the water's height against a small building on the bank of the river near the bridge.

You will begin to climb up a 0.5-mile hill out of North Creek at this point; it is steady, but not steep. After this hill, the terrain levels out for the next 4 miles or so, with gently rolling curves.

As you ride north, you'll begin to notice a bluff in front and to the right of you with a handsome rock face. This is Maxham Mountain.

5.2 *NY 28N bends sharply to the left around a marsh as the road to Olmstedville leads off to the right. Stay left on NY 28N.*

You will begin the second climb of this ride, a moderate rise of about 1 mile, as the road turns left.

Kindred Spirits Adirondack Store in Olmstedville

7.6 *Turn sharply right, around the Minerva Baptist Church, onto the J.P. Morse Memorial Highway, which is also known as County Road 30.*

Now you will reap the benefit of the last climb, with a series of swift descents toward Olmstedville.

8.1 *Continue straight through the intersection.*

If you turn left at this intersection, you will come to the access road for the Minerva Town Beach, on Minerva Lake, just a few tenths of a mile down the road. There is a sandy beach, as well as large, flat rocks perfect for sunning—don't forget your sunscreen—to the left of the beach.

8.7 *Here the steepest descent of the ride begins, for the next mile or so, crossing a bridge.*

10.4 *Cross the bridge over Kelso Brook.*

Notice to the right the dam, which is constructed of wood and stone. In 1804 William Hill built a gristmill at this Olmstedville site.

10.9 *A short, steep climb brings you to the main intersection of Olmstedville; turn right.*

At the corner you will find Kindred Spirits Adirondack Store, which sells maps, camping supplies, packs, guidebooks, gifts, snacks, and drinks. Owners Rick and Christine Beardsley are happy to fill water bottles, brew up a cup of espresso, and chat about the area. The shop also rents mountain bikes, and is the closest thing to a bike shop in the area.

As you ride out of Olmstedville, you will climb the last significant hill of the route, which is not steep, but steady for about .5 mile. On the right you will pass the Minerva Central School.

11.8 *After a sweet descent, turn left onto NY 28N to return to North Creek.*

13.6 *Look out across the gravel pit on the right toward Gore Mountain, which can be identified by the antenna on top.*

15.9 *A last 0.5-mile downhill brings you into North Creek once again.*

16.5 *Cross the Hudson River.*

16.8 *Turn right at the stop sign onto Main Street.*

17.0 *Return to the North Creek Deli and Marketplace.*

19

Speculator: Along the Sacandaga— and a Lot of Other Places, Too

Distance: *77.4 miles*
Terrain: *Moderately rolling to hilly, with a couple of very memorable climbs and descents that can be difficult, but not impossible for the average rider*

This route can be ridden in one long, hard day or broken up into 2 moderate days with camping at Lewey Lake or a hotel in Speculator (try: The Inn at Speculator, 518-548-3811; Melody Lodge, 518-548-6562; or the Adirondack Great Camp, Bearhurst, 518-548-6427). The 2-day option allows more time to browse, hike, canoe, and explore the towns along the way.

0.0 *Begin riding west at the North Creek Deli and Marketplace, with the deli on your right. As you move out of town, note the Hudson River on your right, and the sawmill, which is still in operation along the river.*

0.6 *Turn right onto NY 28.*

There is a generous shoulder along much of this ride, which diminishes the effects of the traffic, much of it trucks, along the route. For the next 5 miles, you will ride within view of the Hudson River.

2.5 *Watch the railroad tracks, which cross NY 28 here at quite a steep angle.*

These tracks are a continuation of the railroad that extended from New York City to North Creek; they travel on to the old iron ore and titanium mine at Tahawus. To your right is a parking area, one of several along this stretch of the route.

4.2 *Enter the town of North River.*

4.4 *Whitewater Challengers, on the left, is one of the best of the many local white-water rafting and kayaking companies that lead tours on the Hudson and other nearby rivers.*

4.5 *Barton Mines Road is on the left.*

This road leads to the still-operating garnet mine of the area. Shaw's General Store, located at the intersection, carries basic foods, fishing gear, and maps of the area. Jasco Minerals, across from Shaw's, has a large collection of rocks, minerals, and fossils, and specializes in native garnet jewelry.

5.1 *Note the parking area on the right, which spans Thirteenth Brook as it joins the Hudson River.*

During the annual canoe and kayak White Water Derby each spring, this is a prime spot to watch the action.

5.5 *The railroad tracks again cross NY 28 at a steep angle. The tracks continue to follow the Hudson River north, as the road pulls away to the west, toward Indian Lake.*

5.8 *You will begin climbing a series of hills as you leave the Hudson.*

None of these climbs is particularly steep, though this first is nearly 2 miles long. As you climb, New York State Bike Route signs will cheer you along.

7.4 *Top of the first hill.*

8.4 *Note the giant chairs on your right, the advertising for Rustic Furniture, which is made here.*

8.8 *Begin the last rise on this series of hills.*

9.5 *This is the top of the climb from North River.*

Now that you're at the top of the ridge, you'll find bogs, meandering streams, and beaver dams along both sides of the road. The woods contain more pine, and are delightfully cool on summer days. The road will continue to be rolling, with smaller hills as you journey west.

13.9 *Note the view to the left of the striking peaks of the Siamese Ponds Wilderness Area, most notably Bullhead Mountain.*

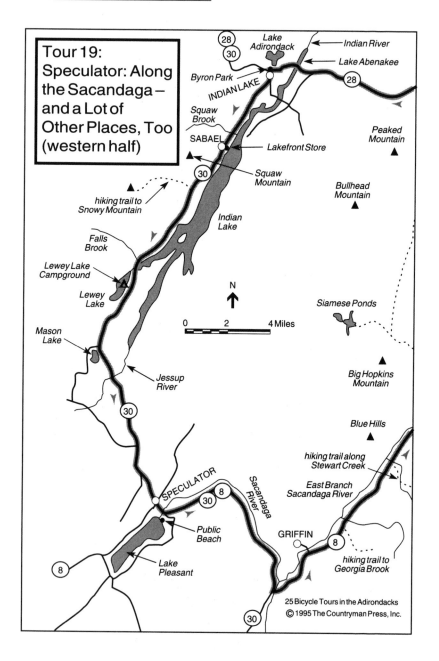

Tour 19:
Speculator: Along the Sacandaga – and a Lot of Other Places, Too (western half)

Lake Adirondack

Indian River

Lake Abenakee

Byron Park

INDIAN LAKE

Squaw Brook

SABAEL

Lakefront Store

Squaw Mountain

Peaked Mountain

Bullhead Mountain

hiking trail to Snowy Mountain

Indian Lake

Falls Brook

Lewey Lake Campground

Lewey Lake

N

0   2   4 Miles

Siamese Ponds

Mason Lake

Jessup River

Big Hopkins Mountain

Blue Hills

hiking trail along Stewart Creek

East Branch Sacandaga River

SPECULATOR

Sacandaga River

Public Beach

GRIFFIN

Lake Pleasant

hiking trail to Georgia Brook

25 Bicycle Tours in the Adirondacks
© 1995 The Countryman Press, Inc.

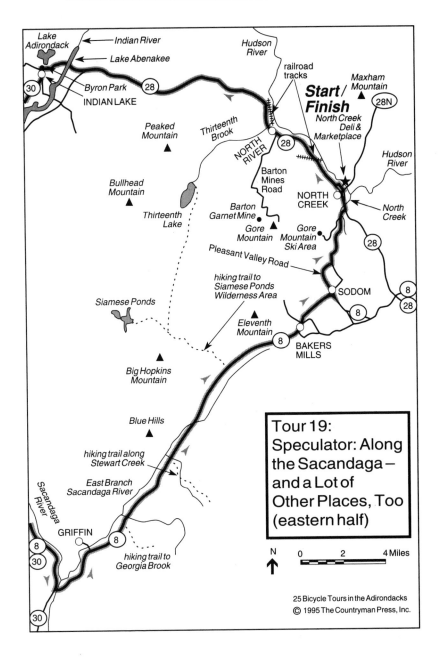

Lake Adirondack

Indian River

Lake Abenakee

Byron Park

INDIAN LAKE

30

28

Hudson River

railroad tracks

Start / Finish

Maxham Mountain

28N

North Creek Deli & Marketplace

Peaked Mountain

Thirteenth Brook

NORTH RIVER

28

Hudson River

Bullhead Mountain

Thirteenth Lake

Barton Mines Road

Barton Garnet Mine

Gore Mountain

Gore Mountain Ski Area

NORTH CREEK

North Creek

28

Pleasant Valley Road

hiking trail to Siamese Ponds Wilderness Area

Siamese Ponds

Eleventh Mountain

8

SODOM

8

8

28

Big Hopkins Mountain

BAKERS MILLS

Blue Hills

hiking trail along Stewart Creek

East Branch Sacandaga River

Sacandaga River

GRIFFIN

8

8

30

hiking trail to Georgia Brook

30

**Tour 19:
Speculator: Along the Sacandaga — and a Lot of Other Places, Too (eastern half)**

N

0   2   4 Miles

25 Bicycle Tours in the Adirondacks
© 1995 The Countryman Press, Inc.

135

14.2 *Begin a steep 0.5-mile descent as you pass the sign for Indian Lake.*

16.0 *Cross Lake Abenakee.*

This is the northernmost body of water connected to Indian Lake, which extends some 12 miles to the south-southwest. The town of Indian Lake claims status as the "Whitewater Capital of the Adirondacks." On most spring and summer weekends it is filled with people wearing wetsuits and looking a little dazed.

To your left, a parking area on Lake Abenakee provides a good place to stop and enjoy the view. As you leave the lake, you will begin climbing a series of short but steep hills into the hamlet of Indian Lake.

16.9 *Lake Adirondack lies on your right, with Byron Park just on the other side of the bridge.*

17.4 *At the junction of NY 28 and NY 30, take a left turn south on NY 30.*

A Grand Union grocery store is on your right. Angelina's Pizza, on your left, has some of the best pizza in the park.

At this intersection, Teddy's Trail splits off going west on NY 28.

17.9 *Begin first uphill.*

18.0 *Note the Indian Lake Ski Center on your right.*

Many communities in the Adirondacks have municipal ski centers, allowing townsfolk without tourist-level dollars to enjoy one of the great benefits of 10-month winters.

18.4 *Pass or pause at the scenic overlook at the top of the hill.*

You can see Bullhead Mountain, Peaked Mountain, and other peaks of the Siamese Ponds Wilderness Area across Indian Lake. As you head down the hill, you can see Snowy Mountain several miles ahead.

19.0 *The bottom of the hill.*

The route becomes quite rolling now. In general, Adirondack lakeshore routes are no guarantee of level riding. Think of it as an incredibly scenic, muscle-powered rollercoaster ride.

21.0 *Cross over Squaw Brook.*

The woods are dense with maple and evergreen. On windless spring mornings the smell is an amalgam of musty, ancient decay and antiseptic pine. It will clear your mind for the ride ahead.

21.5 *Enter Sabael.*

21.7 *The Lakefront Store is on your left.*

If you need anything from Band-Aids to buckshot, this is your last chance to pick it up before Speculator. They have USGS maps, groceries, hardware, pharmaceuticals—even a soda fountain counter and deli.

23.2 *Begin a steep 0.3-mile climb from the waterfront, up the flank of Squaw Mountain.*

24.7 *Pass the parking area for the trailhead to Snowy Mountain.*

25.7 *Note the bogs on your right here at the height-of-land.*

For the next several miles, every hilltop will yield striking views of Indian Lake and surrounding mountain peaks.

28.0 *Pass a parking area. Indian Lake is narrowing as you reach its southern tip.*

29.4 *Pass over the inlet between Indian Lake and Lewey Lake.*

29.7 *Pass the Lewey Lake Public Campground and Day-Use Area.*

This would be a good place to tent if you are camping and planning to cover the Speculator Loop in 2 days. There are excellent sites on both lakes and at Falls Brook (but choose one back from the highway). If you still have the legs for it, ask the ranger for directions for the short hike to a stand of old-growth forest—a rare find in the Northeast.

32.3 *Begin a notable 0.6-mile-long uphill.*

33.9 *Pass a parking area with a view of Mason Lake.*

35.3 *Cross over the Jessup River.*

35.4 *A Bicycle Route sign gently reassures you as you begin another notable 0.7-mile climb. Enjoy the downhill on the other side.*

A note on roadside critters: Keep an eye out for roadkills, and for red efts, those small, fluorescent salamanders that find warm pavement a real treat after a cold night. Red efts may be the single largest vertebrate biomass in the Adirondacks, but it still feels awful to find one or two ground into your high-pressure Michelins.

39.0 *Note the "Snowmobile Crossing" sign.*

39.7 *This is the last uphill pull before Speculator.*

39.9 *You've reached the top of the hill at Melody Lodge.*

Begin the descent into Speculator, which is steep and fast. If you can take your eyes off the road for half a second, there is a very pleasant view of Lake Pleasant.

41.7 *Enter downtown Speculator, originally named Newton's Corners.*

Jack Leadley Jr., a Speculator historian, writes, "People keep asking me how Speculator got its name. There are several conflicting stories about that." Leadley relates how "Speklater" might have been of Native American origin, or coined by the author Charles Webber, or named after two mythic prospectors who died in a blizzard. The truth may never be known, but asking the question of an old-timer in town will surely yield another theory or two.

In her book, *An Adirondack Archive,* Nan Clarkson records this piece, written by William Hudnut at the turn of the century describing Speculator and its environs:

> *Those little Adirondack towns were very much alike: one or two hotels, a general store and post office, a white church (usually Methodist), a blacksmith shop, a school, and a few houses close by the road. In the summer there was some farming in the valleys ... mostly hay and potatoes and patch of corn. The harvest was always uncertain because of the frosts, which could and often did blacken the potatoes by mid-August and sear the corn as if by fire.*
>
> *Many of the men worked as guides, taking "sports," as they called us, to the forest streams and lakes for trout or deer. There were lumbering jobs in the winter and those men were expert woodsmen.*

Today, things aren't that much different. "Sports" on bikes might stop to eat at The Cafe, peek in the Speculator Store, "the most talked about store in the Adirondacks," check out the historic Charles Johns Store, or stop at the visitors center for more possibilities.

41.9 Pass through the intersection where NY 8 and NY 30 merge.

You may wish to turn left here for a detour through the village. Be aware that this is the last chance on the route to get food and water, and it's 35 miles to North Creek.

The pavement quality changes at the intersection from asphalt tarmac to concrete, which means that an otherwise wonderful 10-mile ride downhill is marred by the ka-chunk, ka-chunk of your delicate aluminum wheels bottoming out in expansion joints and minicanyons every 20 feet or so. Assuage your rage with thought of the head engineer consigned for eternity to Biker Limbo, endlessly trueing wheels knocked out of round by his road. Or ride the route with wider tires, which will protect your wheels and your body from the shocks.

Local lore maintains that this stretch of highway was a New York State project, experimenting with new pavement types for the state's highways. Presumably, this type of pavement failed the test, and fortunately has not been used elsewhere in the state.

42.2 King of the Frosties Restaurant.

This is a favorite local ice cream spot.

42.3 The Speculator Volunteer Fire Department is on your left.

The wall on the right of the building is painted with a mural of Lake Pleasant. There are also two doors for what may be the only two public bathrooms in town.

42.4 There is a village beach on your right, with tables and benches for picnicking or just taking a break before the big push back to North Creek.

43.5 The car park on the left offers an informational sign and a good view of the area.

50.6 This is the last downhill of this section, and the steepest.
Notice the view of the Sacandaga River valley, which you have paralleled for a few miles.

51.9 Turn left onto NY 8.

NY 8 leaves NY 30 and heads northeast following the East Branch of the Sacandaga River. The next 25 miles are a rolling uphill grade, which, while never steep, can become taxing over such a stretch. A sign warns "Rough Road Next 20 Miles," but it is much nicer pavement than you have been riding. Do watch out for longitudinal cracks near the side of the road, which can swallow a wheel and damage a tire or bring your bike to an unexpectedly quick stop.

54.4 Note the trailhead to Georgia Brook on your right.

On the left is a dirt road that heads to the ghost town of Griffin. Jeanne Robert Foster, in *Adirondack Portraits*, writes about Griffin's demise before the turn of the century in a poem that begins,

> *Towns die the same as folks; we think we know*
> *The reason—change creeps on—it may be true*
> *But some have roots that bring up new growth,*
> *While others go and hardly leave a trace.*
> *I wonder what Steve Griffin would say now*
> *If he could walk again where Griffin lived,*
> *The town named after him, the lumber king,*
> *Builder of tanneries, a pioneer.*

Many such ghost towns bear silent witness to the Adirondack's past tanning industry, now gone.

55.5 Note the bog on your right.

55.9 Picnic tables and a paved turnoff are on your right.

58.1 At the Warren County line the Blue Hills and Big Hopkins Mountain dominate the skyline on the left.

60.7 Pass a trailhead and cross over Stewart Creek.

65.9 The trailhead on your left leads into the Siamese Ponds Wilderness Area and to Thirteenth Lake and Garnet Hill Lodge and Cross-Country Ski Area.

This is a great ski trail in the winter. Eleventh Mountain dominates your view at this point.

67.6 Treat yourself to the first downhill in nearly 16 miles.

69.2 Roll into Bakers Mills.

69.6 *Bakers Mills's one claim to nightlife, the J&J Foxx Lair Tavern, has what one staffperson calls "Fryolator food." Stop here if you are in dire need of calories.*

71.0 *Begin a 1-mile downhill into the hamlet of Sodom.*

72.0 *Turn left onto Pleasant Valley Road.*

The road may not be marked, but there is a cinderblock community center and a baseball diamond at the intersection. Gore Mountain looms over the area.

73.1 *Begin a 2-mile downhill.*

74.9 *Pass a sawmill on your right.*

75.7 *Pass the entrance to Gore Mountain Ski Resort on your left.*

If this ride didn't seem enough, you can climb the 1.5-mile grade to the parking lot to give your quadriceps one last lactic acid bath.

76.2 *Cross over the North Creek.*

76.4 *Turn left onto NY 28.*

There is a public beach on your left if you need a cooling dunk.

77.0 *Turn right on NY 28N, the Roosevelt–Marcy Trail.*

77.1 *Turn left on Main Street into the village.*

77.4 *Return to the North Creek Deli.*

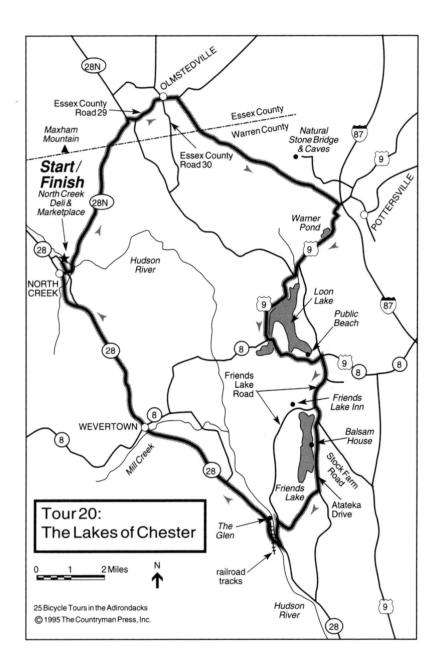

**Start /
Finish**
North Creek
Deli &
Marketplace

28N

Essex County
Road 29

OLMSTEDVILLE

28N

Maxham
Mountain

Essex County

Warren County

Essex County
Road 30

Natural
Stone Bridge
& Caves

87

9

POTTERSVILLE

Warner
Pond

9

28

Hudson
River

NORTH
CREEK

9

9

Loon
Lake

87

Public
Beach

9

8

28

8

9

8

Friends
Lake
Road

Friends
Lake Inn

WEVERTOWN

8

Balsam
House

Mill Creek

Stock Farm
Road

28

Friends
Lake

Atateka
Drive

**Tour 20:
The Lakes of Chester**

The
Glen

0   1   2 Miles

N

railroad
tracks

25 Bicycle Tours in the Adirondacks
© 1995 The Countryman Press, Inc.

Hudson
River

28

9

20
The Lakes of Chester

Distance: 38.5 miles
Terrain: Moderate, with a couple of long, sustained, yet gentle climbs

This loop rolls through the towns of North Creek, Olmstedville, Pottersville, past Loon Lake, Friends Lake, the Hudson River, Wevertown, and back to North Creek. It is a good mix of forest and water, small town and history. Stop at a general store along the way for a drink and a good story.

0.0 **Leave the North Creek Deli and Marketplace, riding east (with the deli on your left) through town.**

Note Braley and Noxon Hardware on your left, which has been in business since the 1880s and has been located in its current building since 1895.

0.2 **Turn left at the stop sign onto NY 28N.**

0.5 **Cross the Hudson River.**

To the right, the North Creek flows into the Hudson under the railroad bridge; to the left, you can see the markers for the water's height against a small building on the bank of the river near the bridge.

You will begin to climb up a 0.5-mile hill out of North Creek at this point; it is steady but not steep. After this hill, the terrain levels out for the next 4 miles or so, with gently rolling curves.

As you ride north, you'll begin to notice Maxham Mountain.

5.2 **NY 28N bends sharply to the left around a marsh. Turn right on County Road 29 to Olmstedville.**

The intersection immediately heads up a short but steep hill.

5.8 **Reach the top of the hill.**

Head down the hill into the hamlet of Olmstedville. See the

Minerva–Olmstedville ride, Tour 18, for details about this community.

6.5 *Pass intersection with County Road 30 in "downtown" Olmstedville.*

6.8 *Pass Betsy's Steak Place on your left.*

6.9 *Bear right at intersection. Follow the "To Interstate 87" sign.*
You will climb a hill through the wooded outskirts of Olmstedville for 0.6 mile, then enjoy a rolling downhill.

8.1 *Enter Warren County.*

10.4 *The road becomes distinctly downhill as you head toward Pottersville.*

11.1 *The downhill becomes a bit more exhilarating.*

13.1 *Bear right at the intersection onto US 9.*
The Pottersville Market is on your right. You can sit down at a table behind the large window, enjoy something cold and wet, and peruse the selection of *National Enquirer* and *Weekly World News* back issues.

Across the street the Lighthouse Baptist Church sits cheek-to-jowl with the area's best-known biker bar. But if you are a biker of the muscle-powered kind, it may be best to savor a beer later on. The clientele is less well known for Lycra, sew-ups, and Italian chromoly than it is for leather, whitewalls, and Harley iron.

13.3 *Pass the Black Bear Restaurant and Lounge on your left.*
Begin a gentle uphill out of Pottersville. If you are in need, there are many campgrounds for the next few miles.

13.9 *Roll by Warner Pond on your right.*
The road, with a moderate shoulder, is gentle and winding along the pond.

16.2 *You can now see Loon Lake on your left; you'll be treated to many beautiful views of this lake over the next couple of miles.*
Loon Lake's shores are dotted with summer camps and rental cabins.

18.1 *Bear left as US 9 splits to join with NY 8.*

The traffic may increase here, and the shoulder gets narrow.

18.2 *At the stop sign, turn left, heading east on NY 8 and US 9.*

As you cross over the bridge that spans the Loon Lake inlet, notice on the right the aquatic birds, lily pads, and occasional splashes from the smallmouth bass and pickerel that haunt this shallow inlet.

19.8 *Pass by the Loon Lake Public Beach on your left.*

20.0 *Turn right onto Friends Lake Road.*

20.7 *Bear right at the fork.*

There may be signs pointing you toward Balsam House and Friends Lake Inn.

21.5 *Bear left at the fork onto Atateka Drive.*

There may be a sign pointing you toward Balsam House.

22.1 *You can glimpse views of Friends Lake on your right.*

23.3 *Pass by an old-fashioned water tower on your left.*

23.8 *Pass Balsam House on your right.*

Balsam House, a century-old inn, is an expensive, fine restaurant. Its bakery, smokehouse, wine cellar, and French country cuisine might lure even the most road-hardened pasta junkie inside for an evening of rich decadence.

On the other side of the lake is the Friends Lake Inn, which this route does not pass by, but which is a favorite of ours. The inn's huge selection of wine, microbrewed beers, and skillfully interpreted regional recipes will charm the palate. Its at-once homey and elegant Adirondack ambiance will relax the road-weary soul.

Both the Balsam House (518-494-2828) and Friends Lake Inn (518-251-4751) have accommodations, although as this book went to press in 1995, the Balsam House was undergoing extensive renovations.

24.2 *Bear right at Circle B Farm.*

Here the road becomes rolling and tends uphill.

25.5 *Hump up a very steep but very short uphill.*

25.7 *Begin a great curvy downhill toward the Hudson River.*

The North Creek Deli and Marketplace, the start and end
of the tours from North Creek

26.0 Turn left at the stop sign onto Friends Lake Road.

You'll roll downstream along the Hudson River for 1 mile.

26.9 Turn right onto NY 28 going north toward North Creek.

The traffic will increase dramatically on this leg of the trip, but the pavement is excellent and the shoulders are wide. The downside is that you are now at the lowest elevation of the route and must now climb back to North Creek to regain all the potential energy you squandered on momentum, air turbulence, and road friction.

27.0 Cross over the Hudson River.

This stretch of the river is called the Glen. Sheer rock walls, playful rapids, deep pools, and giant boulders make it a kayaker's paradise when the water is high. If you're interested in learning how to run the rapids, stop in at Wild Water Outdoor Center, on your left just past the Glen bridge.

27.2 Railroad tracks cross the road at a steep angle.

28.3 The gradual uphill grade becomes steeper for 0.5 mile.

The uphill grade varies from flat to medium steep, but it is long. When you reach the height-of-land in Wevertown, you will have ground out 5 tough miles. Congratulate yourself.

32.2 You've reached the top! Enjoy the downhill to Wevertown.

32.8 Cross over Mill Creek.

32.9 Roll straight through the intersection with NY 8.

You still have some uphill to go before North Creek, but the grade is not steep. Take heart—you'll make it!

33.8 Pass by the White Pine Restaurant, a favorite local breakfast haunt, on your right.

35.8 You've reached the top of the last hill. Roll on into town.

36.7 Go past the carved "Welcome to North Creek" sign.

37.2 Turn right onto Main Street.

38.1 The Goose Pond Inn (518-251-3434), an excellent B&B, is on your right.

38.3 Go straight through the intersection with NY 28N.

38.5 Return to North Creek Deli and Marketplace.

21
Whitewater Challenge

Distance: *23 miles*
Terrain: *Moderate, with rolling hills and a 5-mile stretch of dirt*
Special note: *There are no stores along this route, and only one restaurant (Gallagher's, not always open, at the intersection of NY 8 and US 9, at the 10.4-mile mark); provision yourself in North Creek before you begin!*

Most people think of the Hudson River as it appears near New York City or in the lower Hudson Valley. But the river has it source in the Adirondacks, where it is born in Lake Tear of the Clouds, high on the side of Mt. Marcy, New York's tallest peak. And in these mountains it is not a wide, ponderous, water highway—it is a pounding, steep white-water river, narrow enough that you can chuck a rock from bank to bank.

Above North River, the kayakers and rafters own the river. In the spring, when the water is high, thousands of tourists pay $100 a day for a trip down the rapids, which are among the best in the Northeast. But below North Creek, the land is a little less wild, and more roads begin to appear. This trail follows a dirt road along the south bank of the river most of the way to a bridge crossing in Riparius—most of the time you are a few hundred feet above the rapids, and especially in the spring and late fall, when the leaves are down, it offers terrific views of the river.

After the crossing in Riparius, we leave the river behind for a while, encountering other typical Adirondack landscapes. Loon Lake is a gorgeous small lake, and the road takes you right along the shore. From there we swing up into the second-growth woods with some sweeping mountain views. The ride ends up back in North Creek, where it crosses the Hudson one more time.

This route doesn't really begin at the North Creek Deli, but it's only a

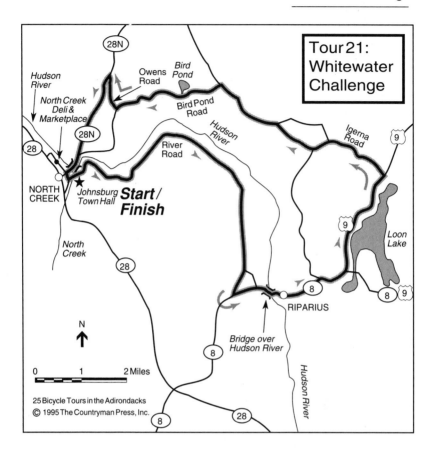

couple of minutes' pedal to its proper start. Just ride east on Main Street through the center of town (past the bank and churches) and through the four-way stop. Shortly after Johnsburg Town Hall, which has plenty of parking, you'll see River Road on the left.

0.0 *Follow River Road south out of town.*

0.3 *River Road turns into a dirt road.*

The road, which is well packed, joins the Hudson at about 0.5 mile, and then climbs to a sign at 1.1 miles which indicates that it is a seasonal-use road and not maintained by the town after November. This is good news for skiers, but for bikes it means the track is no longer so well packed or graded. Watch out for potholes, and stay on either side. The crown of the road, untracked by tires, is soft and sandy, but the sides are mostly passable if you take it slowly—especially on downhills!

By the 2-mile mark you will be high above the river, and when the leaves aren't blocking the way you can see a mile or more upstream. At 2.6 miles you look down on one of the roughest rapids on this stretch of river. Eventually, the road leaves sight of the river, but if you stop pedaling and catch your breath, you can usually hear it in the distance.

5.4   Pavement resumes.

7.6   Turn left onto NY 8.

NY 8 is a busier road, at least by Adirondack standards, and the right shoulder is pretty ragged. Keep your wits about you as you enjoy the long coast down to the river at Riparius. This town used to go by the more prosaic name of Riverside, but when it applied for a post office it learned another New York burg had already claimed the name, so it went for the Latin equivalent. There is no store at Riparius, but there is a post office, and a small parking lot by the bridge that is used as a put-in spot for canoes—it makes scrambling down to the water much easier, and many choose it as a picnic venue.

8.6   Cross the steel-deck bridge on NY 8.

Caution: This bridge is slippery, especially when wet, and walking is recommended. Obey the traffic light too—it's a short light, and so cars sometimes rush to beat it. Watch out! Continue on NY 8 up the hill through Riparius.

10.4   Bear left at the junction with US 9, following US 9 north around Loon Lake.

The shoulder of the road is much better here, which is lucky, since the fine lake views will distract you.

The many small cottages and cabin hotels along this lake are left from an older age of Adirondack tourism. In recent years environmentalists have worked hard, with some success, to slow the development of the region's shoreline and keep more of the lakes wild. There are not many loons on Loon Lake—the shy birds don't much care for people. But many of the remoter lakes in other parts of the park still echo with their weird and lovely call. And some of the other common Adirondack place names are becoming more real again as well—eagles have begun to nest once more within the park, and the moose has slowly started to return, wandering overland from Vermont and Maine.

12.8 Turn left on Igerna Road.

This wide, rolling, and nicely paved road leads past many a collapsed barn and grown-in pasture. In the last century people tried hard to farm the Adirondacks, but the weather made it very difficult—100 days without frost is all you can count on. You can also see evidence of what currently underpins the local economy—the muddy openings in the woods where loggers have been skidding trees out to the road. If there's fresh mud on the pavement by one of these openings, it's a sure tip-off the log job is active.

At 16.4 miles, look west across the meadows to the mountains.

17.2 Just past a cemetery, turn left on to Bird Pond Road.

You'll soon have more fine views to the craggy ledges above the Hudson's north bank, especially once you've passed the Seventh-Day Adventist Church at 19.3 miles.

19.7 Turn right onto Owens Road, and follow it downhill—go slowly and savor the mountain view directly ahead.

20.3 Turn left, uphill on NY 28N.

This is a busier road, and the shoulder is not as wide as it should be, so exercise care.

22.6 Cross the Hudson again, this time on a paved bridge.

The access to the water is not as formal here as it was at Riparius, but it's easy to scramble down the hill.

22.8 Turn left at the stop sign, and follow Main Street 0.2 mile to the beginning of your route at River Road—or turn right and return to the deli.

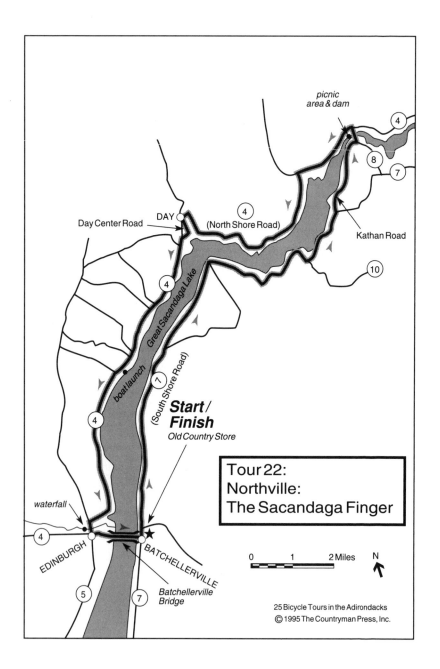

picnic
area & dam

④

⑧

⑦

DAY

Day Center Road → ④ (North Shore Road)

Kathan Road

④

Great Sacandaga Lake

⑩

boat launch

⑦

(South Shore Road)

**Start /
Finish**
Old Country Store

**Tour 22:
Northville:
The Sacandaga Finger**

④

waterfall

④

EDINBURGH

BATCHELLERVILLE

★

*Batchellerville
Bridge*

⑤

⑦

0   1   2 Miles

N

25 Bicycle Tours in the Adirondacks
© 1995 The Countryman Press, Inc.

152

22
Northville: The Sacandaga Finger

Distance: *30 miles*
Terrain: *Gentle*

You are almost never out of sight of water on this easy ride. The western end of the Sacandaga reservoir is almost entirely girdled by road, and though the area is crammed with summer cottages only a few of them have been built between the road and the water. In most places only trees obstruct your view, and often they are mighty pines, whose bare lower trunks merely frame the panorama. There are also open vistas at several spots, where you can look east and south down the reach of the lake.

Sacandaga, gorgeous as it is, is not a natural lake. It may have been more gorgeous once upon a time—*Sac-an-da-ga* meant "land of waving grass" to the native peoples of the Adironadacks, who enjoyed this spot long before it was flooded for a power station in 1930. (It also flooded the fishing retreat of Sir William Johnson, a hero of the French and Indian Wars and one of the first manor lords of the Adirondacks.) The water now covers 26,700 acres, making it second in size only to Lake George among Adirondack waters.

The gently rolling lakeshore roads make this tour ideal for beginning cyclists or for an early season warm-up. There is a drawback, though—almost all the land is privately owned, and because of the number of cottages the traffic can be heavy, at least by Adirondack standards, in the summer. This is especially true on the second half of the ride, when you are using County Road 4, a main thoroughfare. As usual, the shoulders are minimal at best, and the many curves mean you'll need to be very wary if you travel this road at high season. Therefore, we enjoy it most in the spring and in the fall. As an added bonus, the leaves don't block the lake views in those seasons.

Virtually all the land around the lake is private, so only at a few spots can you park your bike and walk down to the water. Luckily, these few oases are set at good distances for lunch and rest—roughly halfway and two-thirds of the way through the trip.

We recommend beginning the tour at the Old Country Store, just north of the southern end of the bridge that crosses the lake at Batchellerville. Coming from the west, follow County Road 149 out of Northville, and then follow signs toward Edinburg—they'll take you right to the bridge. From the west, follow County Road 4 from Hadley. The friendly proprietors of the Old Country Store, which opens at 6 AM, are happy to accommodate bikers' cars until their lot is full. They are also happy to fill water bottles and sell homemade apple pie. (It is the only place to buy provisions on this side of the lake.)

0.0 *Turn right out of the Old Country Store lot, following County Road 7 with the lake on your left. This appears on some maps as South Shore Road.*

The road winds gently along the shore, with almost no elevation to fight as you get your legs warmed up. There is no shoulder until the 7.5-mile mark. However, this side of the lake is less traveled than the other, and it is less nerve-racking. At 8.4 miles, the road crosses a brook feeding the lake, and then climbs momentarily before heading into a lovely few miles of undeveloped land with fine views.

11.3 *Before the crest of a moderate hill, turn left onto Kathan Road.*

The steep downhill takes you right to the lake—the pavement is ragged and bumpy, so control your exuberance.

13.2 *A small park off to the left offers a nice spot for lunch, right at the head of the lake.*

13.3 *Turn left off Kathan Road, and ride across the top of the dam.*

To your right is the power station that taps the power of the reservoir's 33.1 billion cubic feet of water. At times, though, that figure is much smaller. The first time we rode this route, in the fall of 1991, a dry summer had left huge stretches of sand around the edges of the lake—docks rested awkwardly on the sand, 20 feet from the water's edge. Many fishermen use the lake, which is rich in bass and pike.

The bridge over the Sacandaga

13.6 **Turn left, uphill onto County Road 4.**

This road is the busier side of the lake, especially in summer. At 14.2 miles you will pass the Day Country Store, open 8–8 in the summer and 8–6 the rest of the time. It offers sandwiches, and there is a pay phone across the street. At 18.8 miles, at a relatively high spot in the road, a long opening offers a sweeping view down the lake. Customers at Betty and John's Tavern (19.4 miles) enjoy a similar vista.

Cottages line the right side of the road, and it's fun to keep track of their names—Lazy Livin' Lodge is our favorite. In the summer, the clink of horseshoes can usually be heard above the outboards on the lake.

20.4 **Cross the road and go left down Day Center Road, which is unmarked at this end.**

This is a small detour, and if you miss the road don't worry—it rejoins County Road 4 after just 0.3 mile. In the meantime, though, there is a fine view down the lake, and a chance to stop at Day Town Hall and examine the map mounted out front. Across the street from the spot where you rejoin County Road 4 you will find Kennedy's Korners Store.

23.8 **The county operates a boat launch and a small park, which represent the only public access along this side of the route.**

The sign here says "No Bathing," but the rule seems to be largely ignored. From the boat ramp, without even getting your feet wet, you can look down the lake and finally see the bridge that you will cross to end the tour. The route continues past a seasonal ice cream stand at 25.7 miles and a cocktail parlor and dining room at 27.5 miles.

28.0 **Just as the tour is about to end it demands one real climb, a haul that rises 100 feet in 0.5 mile.**

28.5 **Bear left as the hill moderates, crossing a beautiful small brook with a waterfall.**

28.7 **Turn left at the stop sign next to Edinburg United Methodist Church. Caution: It's a somewhat tricky four-way intersection.**

The route will now take you steeply down the hill, an exhilarating freefall that leads to the even more exhilarating bridge crossing. For 0.5 mile across the bridge you are gloriously out in the open, with unlimited views in either direction. Your bike seat will be above the level of the modest guardrail, so there is nothing to interrupt the vista, and the bridge is paved with some novel surface smoother than anything you will have encountered all day. The only drawback is that there's no shoulder. So be extremely careful.

29.9 As soon as you leave the bridge, turn left onto County Road 7. Within 0.1 mile you are back at the Old Country Store, where you have earned a piece of fresh carrot cake.

23
Piseco Lake Loop

Distance: 14.6 miles
Terrain: Gentle, but the pavement can be execrable

Piseco—a lake big enough to absorb motorboats without seeming too spoiled but small enough to circle in less than a few hours of easy pedaling—is a small dot of settlement in one of the park's most deserted regions. NY 8, which makes up a portion of the ride, connects the town of Poland with the village of Speculator, but since neither is an enormous resort the road is not a beaten track.

You are likely to see backpackers along the north side of this loop, covering the 3 miles of pavement that links two sections of the magnificent Northville–Lake Placid Trail, which runs 132 miles from the southern section of the park to the heart of the High Peaks. Some hikers go all the way, on 10- to 15-day jaunts that are small-scale versions of Appalachian Trail through-hikes. Others work on one section at a time—below, at the appropriate spots, we've included some information on what lies north or south of Piseco on the trail in case you're interested in a bikehike outing. (Since the trail goes through designated wilderness areas, however, mountain biking is improper and illegal.) There are other shorter hikes along this route as well, notably the scramble up to the Panther Mountain overlook, which gains 800 feet in a mere 0.75 mile and lets you see the entire route of this trip.

As is often the case with Adirondacks bike trips, do not arrive in Piseco expecting to do extensive provisioning. The general stores offer sodas, loaves of bread, perhaps a jar of peanut butter—for a wider selection, visit the Mountain Market or some of the other stores about 10 miles north of this route in Speculator.

This is a remarkably easy jaunt, perfect for a family trip or for the first

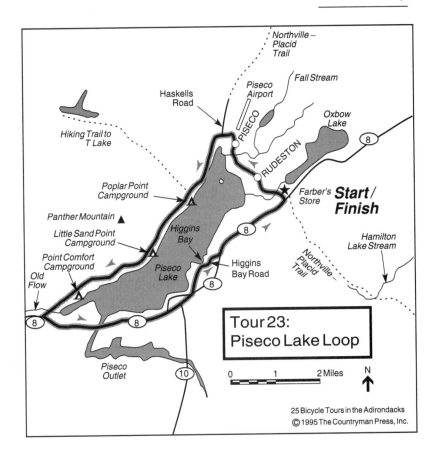

Tour 23:
Piseco Lake Loop

0   1   2 Miles   N

25 Bicycle Tours in the Adirondacks
© 1995 The Countryman Press, Inc.

ride of the spring when you want to stretch your legs but not too far. (In fact, early spring, before the cottagers and their cars have arrived, is a prime time to take this trip in peace.) And it offers superlative camping opportunities at the three state campsites clustered together on the lake's western edge.

Most of the land around the lake is private, but the state campsites provide easy access. Because they are all along the same short stretch, you may want to start from a different point along the route and time your arrival at these sandy public beaches with the lunch hour. Or you may want to begin and end at the state sites, so that you can swim off the slight sweat this lovely tour will produce.

Start the ride at Farber's General Store, on NY 8 north of the junction with NY 10. Farber's is across the street from the town public-works garage, where there never seems to be any trouble with parking—you may see the cars of hikers who have set out along the Northville–Lake Placid Trail. Farber's boasts a kindly clerk and shelves carefully stocked by the American Cholesterol Council.

0.0 *From Farber's, follow the signs to Piseco, downhill and west from NY 8.*

At the bottom of the hill you will pass the outlet from Oxbow Lake, a beautiful body of water just to the north. The marshy outlet hosts a diversity of birds, and often birders with long lenses and spotting scopes can be observed along the road.

0.6 *In the small settlement of Rudeston, you'll pass the Piseco Town Justice and Community Hall, site of summertime suppers and other local events. A bulletin board is out front.*

1.0 *To the left, the sharp face of Panther Mountain is visible.*

1.6 *The road crosses Fall Stream, reputedly a good fishing hole.*

2.0 *Piseco airport comes into view.*

The airport is a story in itself. Several years ago, fearing that the spruce and pine were growing too tall at the end of the runway, the managers proposed to cut them down. But the airport bordered land owned by the state that is "forever wild" under New York's constitution. Not a tree on the forest preserve can be harvested under the constitution unless the legislature votes so in two successive sessions, and then the state's voters approve the idea in a referendum. So that's just what finally happened—along with electing governors and senators, the Empire State's voters finally allowed a few dozen trees at the end of the runway to be cut down.

2.2 *Haskells Road heads off to the right, leading in about 0.8 mile to the next leg of the Northville–Placid Trail.*

If you are interested in a lengthy side trip, this is a fine one, for the NP Trail crosses what is probably its most wild and remote terrain in the sections north of Piseco. The West Canada Lakes Wilderness, 160,000 acres in size, is not particularly steep, but it is dense

Windsurfers on Piseco Lake

and sometimes confusing—a lost hiker starved to death there several years ago, even as hundreds of forest rangers and volunteers mounted an enormous search. A hike of just less than 10 miles will bring you to gorgeous Spruce Lake, with three Adirondack lean-tos along its banks, but it's probably best to carry the Adirondack Mountain Club's pocket guide to the trail to avoid a wrong turn.

2.4 *Just after the pavement turns crummy, you'll pass the Irondequoit Lodge on the left at the top of a rise.*

Having celebrated its centennial in 1992, this inn is now embarked on a second century of providing beautiful views and fine food. For those who don't need a bed, it also offers a private tent campground along the shores of the lake. For reservations call 518-548-5500.

4.0 *After a stretch of shady pedaling past summer houses with clever names (Virginia's Beach), you'll reach the first of three state campsites, at Poplar Point.*

There are bathrooms here, as well as picnic tables, a place to launch boats, and a broad and sandy beach. From the beach, looking to the north and east, you can appreciate the true beauty of this hill-ringed lake: Instead of the steep shores common in more mountainous regions of the park, this lake offers real vistas, at least from this side. Across the road from the campground is a trail to a lean-to at T-Lake, 3.65 miles distant, and 0.2 mile up the road on the left is a canoe livery.

5.0 *Little Sand Point state campsite offers more secluded tent sites, as well as a pay phone across the road.*

5.5 *On the right, a trail leads 0.75 mile steeply uphill to an overlook on Panther Mountain.*

7.0 *The third state campground, at Point Comfort, commands the narrow southern end of the lake.*

7.9 *After crossing the bridge at Old Flow, you'll come to the Piseco Lake Lodge, a less expensive hostelry than the Irondequoit up the road.*

A boat livery offers all manner of fossil-fuel and muscle-powered craft, and a small store sells camping supplies. Cocktails are available as well. For information call 518-548-8552.

8.1 *After climbing a short hill, the road you have been traveling intersects with NY 8. Take a left onto NY 8.*

The road was repaved in the early 1990s and offers a silky riding surface as well as a wide shoulder. As a result, even the decent hill that greets you as soon as you make the turn is conquered with ease, allowing you to look out at the mountains to the north. The highway then stays nearly flat for a long stretch.

9.3 *Cross Piseco Outlet, a good-sized stream that draws anglers.*

As you continue on, the lake is nearby on the left, but hard to see once the trees are in full leaf. You'll notice, among other things, the many beech trees badly scarred by a blight that is decimating the species. The blisters and bulges that this imported pest produce are doing much to change the ecology of the Adirondacks.

11.0 *Pass the junction with NY 10.*

To the south along NY 10 lies some of the loneliest highway in the eastern United States, a 20-mile stretch with little in the way of settlement. If you drive it by car, keep your eyes sharp for wildlife.

11.5 *Just as the new pavement ends, turn left on Higgins Bay Road, which leads back downhill to the lake.*

The road comes right to the water, and though public access is scarce there is a good view back across at the state campgrounds and Panther Mountain.

12.8 *Higgins Bay Road rejoins NY 8. Take a left, and continue along this highway.*

14.6 *You're back to the starting point at Farber's Store.*

On the other side of the road you'll see the familiar brown-and-yellow state sign pointing out the route south on the Northville–Placid Trail. This is a lovely and easy section, leading past a beaver dam to Hamilton Lake Stream, 3.7 miles distant. This is a wonderful place to spend the night, camped by the swinging suspension bridge and lulled to sleep by the rushing water.

24

Old Forge: Deer, Water, Hardware

Distance: *23.4 miles*
Terrain: *Mostly easy, with a couple of moderate climbs*

Most folks know of the Adirondack Park as a place of mountains, but it is justly renowned for its lakes as well. Bordered on the east by Lake Champlain, the park contains many large and small lakes within its boundaries. Many of these lakes feed the park's (and, indeed, New York State's) rivers, and are sought for their beauty, their fish, and the recreational opportunities they offer.

Nestled in the southwestern corner of the park, the Fulton Chain of Lakes is a series of eight lakes that are named, appropriately if not creatively, First through Eighth Lake. The lakes are interconnected, except for a break between Fifth and Sixth Lake, and are a favorite vacation destination for canoeists, fisherfolk, campers, hikers, and other travelers.

This bike loop circumnavigates the body of water that is made up of First, Second, Third, and Fourth Lakes. It begins in the town of Inlet (one end of the Raquette Lake–Inlet ride, Tour 25), travels a winding back road to the town of Old Forge, and returns along the other side of the lakes.

When first entering the town of Old Forge, one is tempted to call it "Lake George West," because of its many tourist attractions, including the Water Safari/Enchanted Forest theme park. However, once you get past the water park and the McDonald's (still a rarity in much of the Adirondacks), the town turns out to be quite charming. There are a variety of restaurants, from fast-food types to diners to places with more elegant fare. Besides the obligatory grocery store, laundromat, and T-shirt shop, several specialized gift shops offer Adirondack crafts, antiques, and imported goods. A personal favorite is Stuff from Other Countries, the store in town that should receive the truth-in-advertising award. There is

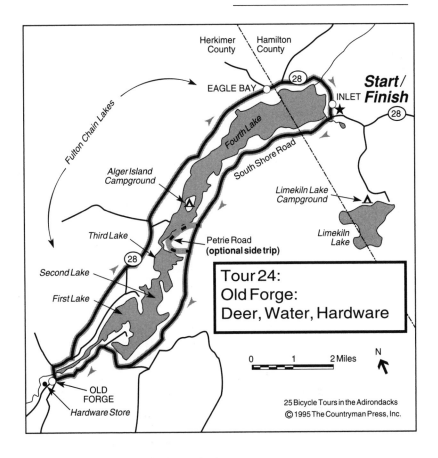

Herkimer County

Hamilton County

EAGLE BAY

28

Start /
INLET **Finish**

28

Fulton Chain Lakes

Fourth Lake

South Shore Road

*Alger Island
Campground*

Limekiln Lake
Campground

Third Lake

Petrie Road
(optional side trip)

*Limekiln
Lake*

28

Second Lake

First Lake

**Tour 24:
Old Forge:
Deer, Water, Hardware**

0   1   2 Miles

N

OLD
FORGE

Hardware Store

25 Bicycle Tours in the Adirondacks
© 1995 The Countryman Press, Inc.

no bike shop, but you will find the Moose River Company Outfitters, which can help you out in a pinch.

The greatest retail treasure of Old Forge, however, is Old Forge Hardware, whose sign boasts "The Adirondack's Most General Store." That might seem a bold claim, especially if you've been in some of the better general stores in the park, but none holds a candle to the sheer variety and volume available here. Betsy Folwell, in her excellent guide *The Adirondack Book,* has this to say about Old Forge Hardware: "Need a pack basket? Bamboo steamer for your wok? Man O' War brand spar varnish? Snowshoes? Inflatable pool? Reflective dog collar to fit a Newfoundland? Authentic shade for your antique Aladdin lamp? Squirrel-baffling bird feeders? Spiles for maple sugaring? Replacement handle for your peavey? You can spend an entire day here." We would only add that there's also a fine bookstore and some of the most beautiful, handcrafted wooden canoes (upstairs, don't miss them!) to be found anywhere. You won't find old-world Campagnolo vintage derailleurs, but that's about all that's missing. You can definitely spend an entire day here.

Traffic in and out of Old Forge (and along NY 28) can be quite heavy during the summer months, especially on weekends. There are narrow shoulders on NY 28, but if you really hate riding in traffic, you may want to return to Inlet along the back road you took to Old Forge, which is usually fairly free of cars and has few, if any, trucks.

Lodging can be found in Inlet, and there is a state campground at Limekiln Lake, about 3 miles east and south of town.

0.0 **Begin the tour at the intersection of NY 28 and South Shore Road in Inlet. Take South Shore Road out of town.**

The intersection is just across from Kalil's grocery and the Inlet Department Store. Just a few doors down is Pedal and Petals, a bike shop and florist all under one roof. It's a good, dependable bike shop that will do repairs at a moment's notice, and owners Ted Christodaro and Cindy Gordon are happy to talk about other good rides in the area.

0.7 **After a remarkably flat section of road—especially for the Adirondacks—the terrain becomes more hilly.**

1.0 **Pass the sign for the Herkimer county line.**

As you ride, the houses become distinctly fancier, looking more like second homes, which is what most of them are. The land on either side of the road is wooded and quiet.

4.5 **The pond on your left is a favorite of fisherfolk in the area, who are often casting directly from the parking area.**

4.8 **The road to the right leads to the ranger's office for the Alger Island Campground.**

The campground itself is actually on an island, and unless you've thought to carry a collapsible canoe with you, you won't be able to get there. However, the detour is worthwhile for the lovely view of Fourth Lake. If you continue past the boat dock, you'll return to South Shore Road at mile 5.3.

Slow deer crossing

167

At about this point on the loop, you may glimpse a deer or two on the side of the road. Ecstatic to catch sight of such wildlife, you stop, stealthily withdraw your camera, turn off the flash, and try to sneak a picture without spooking these graceful creatures ... when it suddenly dawns on you that these deer are hard to spook. In fact, they are quite tame, having grown accustomed to being hand-fed by locals and tourists from their cars. The whitetails are a bit more skittish, but the mule deer (larger and darker than the white-tailed deer) will come right up and nuzzle your hand, expecting food. This is charming or depressing, depending on your opinion of how wild the wildlife in the park ought to be. You're likely to see several more between here and Old Forge. On one recent trip to and from Old Forge on the South Shore Road, a cyclist counted 22 deer in all.

The terrain grows increasingly hilly at this point, with short, steep climbs and equally steep, rapid descents, rather like a roller-coaster.

7.2 *Here you can catch glimpses of First Lake through the trees on your right.*

11.2 *As you begin to come into the town of Old Forge, the trees open to your right, so that you can clearly see not only First Lake, but the Water Safari theme park across the water.*

11.5 *At the fork, bear right to ride along the water.*

A public beach and lovely park offer good places to stop and enjoy the lake.

11.7 *Turn right onto NY 28 to ride back to Inlet.*

If you wish to explore Old Forge and visit the hardware store, turn left. Most of the retail area is less than a mile in this direction.

11.9 *Pass the Water Safari/Enchanted Forest theme park.*

If you want to cool down in a dramatic way, and don't mind the steep admission fee, you might spend a few hours at this tourist park. The water rides vary from simply paddling around a wading pool to the heart-stopping "Killermanjaro," which seems to drop you straight out of the sky into a receiving pool of water.

Now that you're riding on NY 28, the traffic will pick up considerably. There is a small shoulder, though it is rough at times. At about 6 miles from this point, there is a dirt path (an old railroad bed) on the left side of the road that follows NY 28 quite closely for a few miles. If you have a mountain bike, you may wish to ride on the path to avoid the traffic, returning to NY 28 as the path begins to veer away.

12.5 *A KOA Kampground is on the left.*

14.5 *A small pond opens on your left; in the autumn, it is quite spectacular as it reflects the red and yellow maples on its shore.*

18.3 *You'll begin to catch views of Fourth Lake here, and for much of the rest of the ride.*

20.9 *Enter the small town of Eagle Bay, which offers a general store and a couple of restaurants.*

21.3 *Pass the Hamilton county line sign.*

22.7 *Cross a stream that feeds into Fourth Lake.*

23.2 *Enter the town of Inlet.*

23.4 *Return to the intersection of NY 28 and South Shore Road.*

25

South from Raquette Lake: Woods and Water

Distance: *23.3 miles*
Terrain: *Relatively flat, with a difficult hill near the start and miles of dirt road that will need knobby tires*

Raquette Lake, an island-studded lake in the west-central Adirondacks where this tour begins and ends, is a hauntingly beautiful place. Its wide sheet of water (uncommon in a park where the lakes tend to be steeply lined) offers a gentle vista to the north and west, where mountains and high ridges rise in pleasant profusion. This the largest natural lake in the Adirondacks, and there is a softness to the view that has drawn visitors summer after summer. W.H.H. "Adirondack" Murray, the Boston cleric who set off a 19th-century tourism boom in these mountains with his descriptions of their beauty and bracing air, called it "one of the best water views in the world," and we cannot disagree.

Raquette is one of the park's smallest and most isolated towns. It maintains its own tiny public school and library, but 9 months of the year commerce is highly limited—it is definitely smart to provision elsewhere for your trip, perhaps down the road in Eagle Bay or Inlet. In fact, many riders may choose to start their tour down the road and head north to Raquette Lake, timing their lunch break so they can eat along the boat dock, staring out at the water or taking a swim. There are also boats to rent from several canoe and motorboat liveries, not to mention a dinner cruise aboard the *W.W. Durant,* which will take you past several of the magnificent Great Camps, and—during the summer—the chance to ride the mail boat, which still makes it rounds to the isolated camps and cottages scattered along 99 miles of lakeshore.

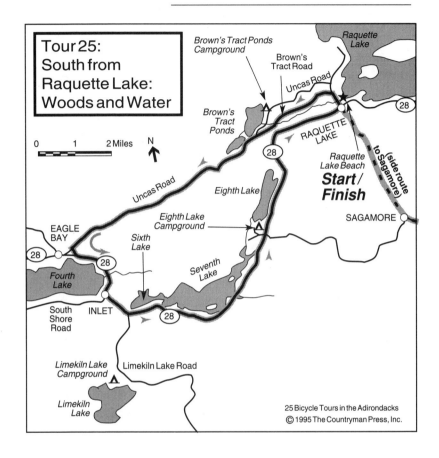

Tour 25:
South from
Raquette Lake:
Woods and Water

Brown's Tract Ponds Campground

Brown's Tract Road

Raquette Lake

Uncas Road

0   1   2 Miles   N

Brown's Tract Ponds

RAQUETTE LAKE

Uncas Road

Raquette Lake Beach

Start / Finish

28

(side route to Sagamore)

Eighth Lake

EAGLE BAY

Eighth Lake Campground

SAGAMORE

28

Sixth Lake

28

Fourth Lake

Seventh Lake

South Shore Road   INLET

28

Limekiln Lake Campground

Limekiln Lake Road

Limekiln Lake

25 Bicycle Tours in the Adirondacks
© 1995 The Countryman Press, Inc.

0.0 *Begin at the boat dock in downtown Raquette Lake, just in front of Raquette Lake Supply and the jewelbox library. Take a right out of town, keeping the library on your left, and ride up the hill that winds out of town.*

0.3 *Turn left on Brown's Tract Road, a sandy dirt road through a thick spruce woods.*

The first 2 miles of this road are by far the softest and most difficult surface you will encounter—try to stick to the crown of the road for slightly easier riding, but be prepared for the occasional push.

1.2 *Shortly after passing under a cedar tree that leans perilously* *out over the road, you will encounter a steep uphill grade.*

The next 0.3 mile feature the only pavement for the next 8 miles, put there because the hill is so steep that dirt would quickly erode away. The pavement is a mixed blessing, tempting you to ride this very steep climb—it can be done if you hunker down in granny gear and push.

1.5   *The pavement ends, just before a downhill that demands full attention since the road remains sandy and rocky.*

2.3   *The office for the lovely Brown's Tract Ponds Campground, a popular summer camping spot administered by the state's Department of Environmental Conservation (315-354-4412).*

The two Brown's Tract Ponds are linked bodies of water in this remote and wooded stretch. Canoes and rowboats can be rented at the campground; powerboats are forbidden.

2.9   *Cross the outlet to the lower pond.*

3.2   *The road begins to improve somewhat here, and you also start to encounter the first of the cottages and summer camps that will line the road much of the way to Eagle Bay.*

This road was built in the late 1800s, and many of its tiny camps recall an earlier day of Adirondack tourism, something in between the city swells of the Great Camp period and the condo-crazed speculators of the present day. The road continues on a lovely level grade for the next 4 miles, almost always shaded by the trees that in some cases nearly arch across the narrow road.

9.2   *On your left you will see a stable, Adirondack Saddle Tours, which offers backcountry rides for fishing, hunting, and camping.*

9.4   *Uncas Road (the name for the second half of this long dirt stretch you have been riding) intersects NY 28, just north of Eagle Bay.*

Turn right for a brief detour to the supermarket that you will find at 9.7 miles, and then head north on NY 28 into Hamilton County.

10.1 *A decent hill, but on fresh pavement in 1994 it was no sweat, especially after the harder rolling along the dirt.*

11.4 *Fourth Lake Outlet.*

For the remainder of this ride you will be passing along the Fulton Chain of Lakes, named—or should we say numbered—First Lake through Eighth Lake, and stretching from Old Forge north toward Raquette. The lakes are very popular as a connected canoeing route with minimal portaging, and quite beautiful though (especially at the southern end) heavily developed.

11.9 *The public park and municipal building in the vacation hamlet of Inlet.*

Almost any weekend night during the summer, you can catch a lecture here on some aspect of Adirondack history or culture, part of the parkwide Adirondack Experience series.

12.1 *Pedals and Petals, a cyclery and florist, with the only repair shop for many, many, many square miles (see Tour 24).*

12.3 *On the left, as you are leaving town, the Mountainman Outdoor Supply store, a wonderful camping store that also rents Diamondback mountain bikes by the day.*

Whatever outdoor supplies you may have forgotten can be purchased here from the knowledgeable owner, John Nemjo, who donates a chunk of his profits to the environmental movement.

12.7 *On your right you will pass Limekiln Lake Road, an important access route into the Moose River Plains.*

Sixth Lake is on your left now as you ride, and then the road to Seventh Lake, and then Seventh Lake itself.

14.3 *You will pass the Seventh Lake House restaurant, one of the last dining possibilities until you reach Raquette Lake (which is not precisely full of eating opportunities).*

15.5 *A turnout on the left offers a view of Seventh Lake.*

16.1 *Crossing a neck of Seventh Lake, a small parking lot offers access for putting in boats, and a place to rest before an uphill push.*

18.1 *The road to the Eighth Lake Campground is visible on the left.*

There is good swimming here, as well as canoe and rowboat rentals, and even showers. If you're making reservations, a 3-day minimum stay is required, but during the week drop-ins can often be accommodated.

22.9 *Turn left to return the 0.4 mile to Raquette Lake.*

If you're up for some more riding, turn right instead on the dirt road that leads, after 4 miles of fairly steep up-and-downs—to the Sagamore Lodge, one of the finest extant examples of Adirondack Great Camp architecture. Built in 1897 by W.W. Durant, it was sold at the turn of the century to Alfred G. Vanderbilt Jr. The Vanderbilts did most of their vacationing in Newport, but when a rustic mood struck they would head for the North Woods, where a small army of servants kept their digs in good repair. Today the complex (with its own open-air bowling alley!) is open for tours and is often used for weekend workshops and craft classes. You can stay there as well: phone 315-354-5311. This is one Adirondack experience not to be missed.

23.1 *As you ride back into Raquette Lake, at a marshy low point in the road you should get off your bike and take time to relish the unforgettable view northeast to Blue Mountain, a promise of further adventures.*

23.3 *Return to the boat dock.*

Let Backcountry Guides Take You There

Our experienced backcountry authors will lead you to the finest trails, parks, and back roads in the following areas:

50 Hikes Series

50 Hikes in the Maine Mountains
50 Hikes in Southern and Coastal Maine
50 Hikes in Vermont
50 Hikes in the White Mountains
50 More Hikes in New Hampshire
50 Hikes in Connecticut
50 Hikes in Massachusetts
50 Hikes in the Hudson Valley
50 Hikes in the Adirondacks
50 Hikes in Central New York
50 Hikes in Western New York
50 Hikes in New Jersey
50 Hikes in Eastern Pennsylvania
50 Hikes in Central Pennsylvania
50 Hikes in Western Pennsylvania
50 Hikes in the Mountains of North Carolina
50 Hikes in Northern Virginia
50 Hikes in Ohio
50 Hikes in Michigan

Walks and Rambles Series

Walks and Rambles on Cape Cod and the Islands
Walks and Rambles in Rhode Island
More Walks and Rambles in Rhode Island
Walks and Rambles on the Delmarva Peninsula
Walks and Rambles in Southwestern Ohio
Walks and Rambles in Ohio's Western Reserve
Walks and Rambles in the Western Hudson Valley
Walks and Rambles on Long Island

25 Bicycle Tours Series

25 Mountain Bike Tours in the Adirondacks
25 Bicycle Tours in Maine
30 Bicycle Tours in New Hampshire
25 Bicycle Tours in Vermont
25 Mountain Bike Tours in Vermont
25 Bicycle Tours on Cape Cod and the Islands
25 Mountain Bike Tours in Massachusetts
30 Bicycle Tours in New Jersey
30 Bicycle Tours in the Finger Lakes Region
25 Bicycle Tours in the Hudson Valley
25 Bicycle Tours in the Twin Cities and Southeastern Minnesota
30 Bicycle Tours in Wisconsin
25 Mountain Bike Tours in the Hudson Valley
25 Bicycle Tours in Ohio's Western Reserve
25 Bicycle Tours in Maryland
25 Bicycle Tours on Delmarva
25 Bicycle Tours in Coastal Georgia and the Carolina Low Country
25 Bicycle Tours in and around Washington, D.C.
25 Bicycle Tours in the Texas Hill Country and West Texas

We offer many more books on hiking, fly-fishing, travel, nature, and other subjects. Our books are available at bookstores and outdoor stores everywhere. For more information or a free catalog, please call 1-800-245-4151 or write to us at The Countryman Press, PO Box 748, Woodstock, Vermont 05091.